PENGUIN BUSINESS
THE STORYPRENEUR'S PLAYBOOK

Nitin Babel is a two-time entrepreneur. He has been recognized by *Forbes* Asia as 30 Under 30 and as a Young Alumni Achiever by IIT Kharagpur. While growing up, Nitin heard his parents' cautionary tales about the hardships of running a business. Still, he persevered and at the age of twenty-five, he co-founded an AI venture, which received funding from Ratan Tata. Post-pandemic, Nitin ventured into his second startup. In 2022, he felt inspired to write about the authentic stories of modern entrepreneurs. Through this book, he hopes to offer budding entrepreneurs a realistic and 360-degree perspective on starting-up.

Prateek Roy Chowdhury grew up in the Himalayas, immersed in stories that fuelled his passion for storytelling. His penchant for narratives—powered by countless *Amar Chitra Katha*s—eventually led him to IIT Kharagpur, where he developed an enduring dedication for psychology and mentorship. Now an HR leader at a multinational corporation, Prateek guides future leaders and entrepreneurs in their startup journey. He believes stories have the power to alter destinies and through this book, he aims to help aspiring entrepreneurs find purpose and meaning.

ADVANCE PRAISE FOR THE BOOK

'*The Storypreneur's Playbook* is an inspiring guide to building a business through the power of storytelling. Nitin and Prateek weave together insights from entrepreneurs with the hero's journey, making this a must-read for anyone ready to take the leap and shape their own success story. Engaging, insightful, truly motivating and I'm so honoured to be a part of it!'—**Alicia Souza, entrepreneur**

'A compelling narrative that intertwines storytelling with entrepreneurial wisdom. If you're on the edge of starting up, this book will give you the nudge you need!'—**Phanindra Sama, founder, redBus**

'Nitin and Prateek's book is not just about starting a business—it's about embarking on a hero's journey. It's a must-read for anyone trying to script their own story'—**Biswapati Sarkar, screenwriter and producer**

THE STORYPRENEUR'S PLAYBOOK

FIFTEEN INSPIRING STORIES TO UNLEASH THE ENTREPRENEUR IN YOU

NITIN BABEL
PRATEEK ROY CHOWDHURY

PENGUIN
BUSINESS

An imprint of Penguin Random House

PENGUIN BUSINESS

Penguin Business is an imprint of the Penguin Random House group of companies
whose addresses can be found at global.penguinrandomhouse.com

Published by Penguin Random House India Pvt. Ltd
4th Floor, Capital Tower 1, MG Road,
Gurugram 122 002, Haryana, India

First published in Penguin Business by Penguin Random House India 2025

Copyright © Nitin Babel and Prateek Roy Chowdhury 2025

ISBN 9780143473671

Typeset in Garamond by MAP Systems, Bengaluru, India
Printed at Thomson Press India Ltd, New Delhi

www.penguin.co.in

*To our alma mater, IIT Kharagpur, where we met
and started our hero's journey*

Contents

Introduction

You are seven years old, and it is the summer vacation of 1994. While you would normally be bound by a set routine any other time of the year, summers bring their own delights. The rest of the year is spent in school, doing homework, sleeping and repeating the cycle—but in summer, you find yourself spending an entire day reading back-to-back *Amar Chitra Katha*s and no one would judge you for it. You have read all the myths and stories of the olden times and imagine yourself in them. You feel the magic, dilemma and glory of their worlds! Rama setting off south to find his Sita, Achilles seeking glory on the beach of Troy, Buddha leaving home to find enlightenment or Prithviraj Chauhan whisking off Samyukta from Kannauj. We were enamoured by the stories of these diverse heroes.

How I would imagine myself as one of these heroes, getting this call to adventure. It was a vision of destiny seeking you, setting out on a journey that would change you and the world with you. I would think of one of these heroes, connect the events of my life with them and feel special—a part of something bigger, as if an adventure would one day appear on my doorstep! As we grow old, life throws us varied choices—stay on the trodden path or be a hero. And there is the proverbial fork in the road. The trodden path will give you stability and comfort but comes at the price of an opportunity lost. On the flip side, if you pick an unknown adventure, it more often than not will show you the path to your unfulfilled destiny.

As I grew up, I discovered Joseph Campbell, an American writer, who worked with comparative mythology. His philosophy was encompassed in the oft-repeated phrase: 'Follow your bliss.' George Lucas of the *Star Wars* movies fame credits the story of his films to Joseph Campbell's influence. Campbell, in his writing, describes a number of stages or steps along the journey of becoming a hero. 'The hero's adventure' begins in the ordinary world, which he must depart when he receives a call to adventure. With the help of a mentor, the hero will cross a guarded threshold, leading him to a supernatural world, where familiar laws and order do not apply. There, the hero will embark on a road of trials and temptations, where he or she is tested along the way. As the hero faces trials, he encounters the greatest challenge of the journey. Upon rising to the challenge, the hero will receive a reward, or a boon. Campbell's theory of the monomyth continues with the inclusion of a metaphorical death and resurrection. The hero must then decide to return with this boon to the ordinary world. Upon the hero's return, the boon or gift may be used to improve the hero's ordinary world, in what Campbell calls 'the application of the boon'. Heroes often find the way back home with the boon, whether it is Frodo in *The Lord of the Rings*, or Lord Rama after vanquishing Ravana to return to Ayodhya, or Mother Teresa finding her calling to uplift the destitute of Kolkata.

While the hero's journey is not limited to myths alone, one vocation that closely epitomizes the pattern of this journey is that of entrepreneurs. The word 'entrepreneur' literally means 'adventurer', much like the sailors who used to invest in ships to find unknown lands to trade with—what has shaped much of the world today. It is interesting to see how entrepreneurs today follow a similar path. Especially in India, one of the world's most exciting startup ecosystems, a startup is born every day! And behind every startup is one entrepreneur or a group of entrepreneurs ready for their hero's journey. Let's take for example Mayank Jain, founder of an agri-tech venture called SumArth. He wanted to fix the broken supply chain of food in the country. Having served three years in the corporate culture, he heard his call to adventure. Mayank overcame the threshold of informing his family and moving to a village in Gaya, Bihar. He faced multiple trials and tribulations, including lack of financial security, family concerns and seeing many of his colleagues give up the challenges of social entrepreneurship. What was special about Mayank was hearing the call and following his bliss. He had to amplify the part of him that was telling him he is the protagonist of his journey. That's what set him apart from so many others, who wanted to but could not take that first step.

As Campbell says, 'If you follow your bliss, you put yourself on a kind of track that has been there all the while, waiting for you, and the life that you ought to be living is the one you are living.'[1]

As we set out to delve deeper into the psychology behind entrepreneurship and that elusive bliss, we find

---

[1] Joseph Campbell, *The Power of Myth*, ed. Betty Sue Flowers (New York: Doubleday, 1988), 120.

that while the stories we know on social media are all fist-pumping and inspiring, in reality, the rubber hits the road hard. What happens beneath the surface is so much more than what is visible. While we all know the Insta-worthy stories featured as *Forbes* 30 Under 30, the real journey is between the lines. The entrepreneur goes through a very personal evolution, much akin to the hero's journey. They set out into the night like the Buddha, often not knowing where the journey will take them, but they know they must go. According to Professor Howard H. Stevenson of Harvard Business School, 'Entrepreneurship is the pursuit of opportunity beyond resources controlled.'[2] A hero pursues his or her destiny beyond what they can control and goes forth to seek that bliss. That their spirit needed to pursue something beyond controlled resources is what distinguishes and rewards heroes. All entrepreneurs, much like the heroes of yore, are faced with the dilemma of whether they should dare or stay within the limits of their circumstances. For those who dare, Campbell says, 'The universe will open doors where there were only walls.'[3]

---

[2] Howard H. Stevenson, *'A Perspective on Entrepreneurship'*, Harvard Business School Working Paper 9-384-131 (Boston: Harvard Business School, 1983).
[3] Joseph Campbell, *The Power of Myth*, ed. Betty Sue Flowers (New York: Doubleday, 1988).

In this book, across six chapters, we explore the journey of over fifteen Indian entrepreneurs of the last decade, who go through the same stages of the hero's journey. This ranges from the adventures of Devashish Chakravarty, an Indian Army major turned entrepreneur, to Sangeeta Saxena, founder of defence magazine Aviation Defence Universe (ADU), who started her entrepreneurial venture at the age of fifty. The heroes include Biswapati Sarkar, who delved into his creativity in The Viral Fever (TVF) and Posham Pa Pictures, to Phanindra Sama, who missed a bus, spurring him into founding one of the biggest success stories of the Indian startup ecosystem—redBus.

Through our conversations, we have distilled the wisdom of many such inspiring entrepreneurs, who have created businesses in various domains, such as technology, travel, media, entertainment and social impact. With the advent of a huge Indian middle class in the first two decades of the twenty-first century, a generation finds itself more hopeful, pragmatic and willing to take risks, unlike their parents who had limited options. We will examine how they have followed their passion, pursued their vision and overcome difficulties encountered along the way. We will also learn from their insights, strategies and lessons that can inspire and guide aspiring entrepreneurs to embark on their own journeys. We hope the book will help entrepreneurs relate to their own story at any stage of their journey—whether they are starting off with a 'call to adventure', getting pushed back in 'trials and temptations' or reflecting on the arc of their 'transformation'. We hope it will inspire everyone who reads the book to start their own story of entrepreneurship, with a fresh 'call to adventure'.

This book is a collection of stories and a framework for understanding and applying the principles of the hero's journey to your own entrepreneurial endeavours. Whether you are an aspiring or struggling entrepreneur, or simply curious about the stories of Indian entrepreneurs, we hope this book will offer you inspiration for your own journey. This book is an attempt to understand the journey about the psychology of entrepreneurship, what lies beneath the surface of the leap of faith—not in a preachy kind of way (hopefully!) but in a way that holds your hand and takes you on a guided tour of what you could be, if you choose to be the protagonist of your story.

Profile of Entrepreneurs

We have selected individuals who are relatable, to the extent that you can easily visualize them living in your neighbourhood. They hardly had anything given to them on a silver platter, but still they decided to go on their 'hero's journey'.

Alicia Souza

Alicia Souza has been referred to as a 'happiness illustrator', owing to the snippets of happy incidents, funny conversations and daily life musings that she draws. Alicia was born and raised in the Middle East; she currently works and lives in Bengaluru with her husband, dog, lots of pencils and most recently, a little human. She gained popularity through her charming illustrations that often depict humorous and everyday situations, featuring characters like animals, monsters and humans. She has a huge following on social media and owns one of the most relatable brands that goes by her name.

Ankit Jain

Ankit Jain is a seasoned social impact consultant. He is a co-founder of GDi Partners, a fast-growing social impact consulting startup, and aspires to solve some of the most compelling and complex problems in this sector. He holds a unique distinction in the experience of having worked at various levels of India's social impact ecosystem— district administration, state departments, the Chief Minister's Office, Central government, think tanks and philanthropies.

As a co-founder at GDi, Ankit leads consulting engagements with governments, philanthropies and non-profits across various domains like air pollution, public sector education, agriculture, livelihoods and digital governance, in various geographies, including Delhi, Punjab, Haryana, Uttar Pradesh and Odisha. He also leads various aspects of organization-building, including business development, talent management and internal processes design.

Before co-founding GDi, Ankit did brief stints with two leading philanthropies in India—Children's Investment

Fund Foundation (CIFF) and Central Square Foundation (CSF). Prior to that, as part of governance consulting firm Samagra Governance, Ankit led teams for design and implementation of public education transformation programmes across states and for wide-ranging reforms as a consultant to the Chief Minister's Office in Haryana.

Ankit graduated from IIT Kharagpur; his decisions and working style reflect his love for science, which he considers a key instrument of social change.

Biswapati Sarkar

Biswapati Sarkar is a screenwriter, actor and producer working with Posham Pa Pictures, the creators of Netflix shows like *Maamla Legal Hai* and *Kaala Paani*. He has written several successful web series like *Kaala Paani*, *Pitchers* S1 and *Permanent Roommates* S1 and S2, besides films like *Jaadugar*, *Fighter* and the upcoming *Logout*. He gained prominence as one of the early members of the popular Indian comedy collective The Viral Fever (TVF).

Devashish Chakravarty

Devashish Chakravarty is an ex-army major, international sportsman, gold medallist MBA from IIM Ahmedabad, and now an entrepreneur, mentor and author—all in the jobs and career space. He runs companies in the HR space, offering employee background verification through QVerify and job loss assurance through SalaryNext. He is a mentor and executive coach to startup founders, seasoned professionals and sportspersons—and author of *Get Hired in 30 Days* and *101 Tough Interview Questions*. He has been the columnist on careers with the *Economic Times* for fifteen years.

Devashish holds the unique distinction of being UPSC Rank 1 for selection to the National Defence Academy and 100 percentile in CAT for selection to IIM Ahmedabad. He has been an accomplished sportsman across multiple sports and adventure sports, having participated in national and international championships in three sports—sailing, shooting and bridge—and has also been an ultra-marathoner. Devashish chose to be part of the book to inspire readers to push their boundaries and inform readers who consider entrepreneurship or startups as a career choice.

Dharamveer Singh Chouhan

Dharamveer Singh Chouhan (DV) is the visionary co-founder and CEO of Zostel, India's first and largest backpacker hostel chain, which has transformed travel across India with its vibrant, community-driven approach. Founded in 2013, Zostel was born from DV's dream to create more than just affordable accommodations— it's a place where travellers connect, share stories and experience destinations through genuine community spirit. Under DV's leadership, Zostel has become a movement, redefining how people engage with travel and with each other. Now, with his latest venture, Zo World, DV is bringing this vision to a global scale. Through a network of Zostels, Zo Houses and immersive Zo Trips, DV is building a world where people can explore like locals, guided by a passionate community that blurs borders and turns every journey into an experience of belonging. For DV, Zo World isn't just about travel; it's about creating a future where everyone feels at home, anywhere.

Mayank Jain

Mayank Jain is the co-founder of SumArth. He is a seasoned entrepreneur with over twelve years of experience working in agriculture and livelihoods, agritech, farmtech and hi-tech industries. Through his work, he has helped in shaping three climate-resilient agriculture-related policies/ practices and has directly impacted more than half a million lives through work interventions, contributing to social, economic and environmental impact in a positive way. With exposure to the innovation ecosystems in the US, Israel and South Korea, the social economy system in South Korea and grassroots learnings in most backward areas of India, he addresses problem-solving through novel approaches that can be seen in his work. His motto, which he is bringing to life through his organization SumArth, is 'Desh ka Culture, Agriculture'.

Mayur Sontakke

Mayur Sontakke, a passionate entrepreneur and community builder, founded NomadGao with a vision to foster human connection and sustainable living. Through his work, he's creating inspiring spaces, where people can connect with nature, collaborate with like-minded individuals and live fulfilling lives. Mayur is a homeschooling father of three; he believes in the combined power of community living and technology to create a more sustainable, equal and fulfilling world. He currently lives in Dharamsala, Himachal Pradesh.

Mehul Jain

Mehul Jain is the founder of Finigami, a cutting-edge fintech startup aimed at revolutionizing financial services through technology. Having been an exceptional academic achiever, he secured an All India Rank of 5 in the IIT-JEE exam. He has a computer science undergraduate degree from IIT Bombay (2011) and an MBA from INSEAD (2015).

Mehul has spent the majority of his professional career (six-plus years) as a business consultant at Kearney, advising corporates across the globe on a range of management problems. He left Kearney as a manager in 2018 to join Guild Capital as vice president investing in and managing a portfolio of early- to mid-stage startups operating in D2C products and SaaS.

Nihal Ahmed

Nihal Ahmed is the founder of Limitless Institute, which creates transformative experiences and tools to help people grow intellectually, emotionally and purposefully, enabling them to lead richer, healthier and more impactful lives. He has developed programmes for everyone, from babies to grandparents. Nihal also founded Ikiguide, a platform that guides individuals to discover their purpose. Known for his unconventional approach, he combines play, immersive learning and the concept of 'ikigai'—one's reason for being—to foster self-discovery and professional development.

Nihal also designs global entrepreneurship programmes, accelerators and fellowships to help individuals turn their ideas into reality. Working closely with a network of creators, artists and ecosystem builders, he focuses on solutions that empower marginalized communities. Recently, he's been working on 'beVisioneers: The Mercedes-Benz Fellowship', which equips young innovators with training, expert guidance and resources to develop impactful, planet-positive projects.

Phanindra Sama

Phanindra Sama is an Indian entrepreneur best known as the co-founder of redBus, India's largest online bus ticketing platform. Born in Nizamabad, Telangana, Phani completed his engineering degree in electrical and electronics engineering from BITS Pilani in 2002. In 2006, while he was working at Texas Instruments,

Sama had a frustrating experience booking a bus ticket to his hometown. This experience inspired him to start redBus along with two friends in 2006. Soon, redBus revolutionized the way bus tickets were booked in India by providing a convenient online platform for users to search for, compare and book bus tickets across various routes. Phani led redBus through a successful exit, making it one of the most well-known success stories of startups in India.

Samarth Mahajan

Samarth Mahajan is a Mumbai-based film-maker, passionate about telling human stories that remain invisible to the mainstream. Having gone to IIT and landed a dream job, he always felt something was missing. He quit his job overnight and moved to Mumbai to make films. His work includes two National Award-winning documentaries—his latest feature *Borderlands* explores lives defined by India's borders, while the 2017 film *The Unreserved* captures stories from the general compartments of Indian Railways.

Samarth has a lot of friends who have wanted to take a leap of faith towards their dream career but are somehow chained by the deep-rooted conditioning that makes us fear both novelty and failure. When Nitin and

Prateek approached him with the idea of their book, he felt two things—firstly, that it would be a solid nudge for people sitting on the fence, and secondly, it would serve as a refreshing perspective for those seeking to know more beyond tried and tested career paths.

Sangeeta Saxena

Sangeeta Saxena, founder and editor of Aviation and Defence Universe (ADU), is recognized globally as one of the prominent voices in defence and aerospace journalism. At fifty, while many consider slowing down, Sangeeta embarked on an inspiring new journey by establishing her own media venture, an online news portal on aerospace and defence. She has to her credit the first book on defence journalism in India, which is a reference book at many universities, both in India and abroad. With over three decades of journalistic experience, her career is marked by live reporting, intensive interviewing and commitment to the tenets of journalism. She has reported from war zones, insurgency-hit regions, militancy-torn states and volatile international borders. Sangeeta's work ensures that she lives out of a suitcase and continues to travel globally, passionately reporting on aerospace and defence matters, covering air, land and naval shows. This is while nurturing her dynamic startup, building it strongly on the foundation of truthful and ethical journalism. Her passion is defence journalism; knowing it is going to be a long march, she believes that she can hold on till the end, standing firm on ADU's motto: 'We Just Report Facts, We Don't Change Them'.

Shishir Modi

Shishir Modi has been an entrepreneur, who has experienced the ups and downs of building startups from ground up—having co-founded Niki.ai, running it for six years and later joining the leadership team of KarmaLife as its chief growth officer. He was recognized by *Forbes* Asia 30 under 30 and was also awarded the Young Alumni Achiever Award by IIT Kharagpur. Through this book, he is excited about the idea of bringing real entrepreneurial experiences to budding founders, helping shape their path for the better.

Vijayananda Prabhu

Vijay has co-founded and grown Linger Leisure, a chain of curated guest houses and farm stays, that offers a unique and memorable vacation experience. Linger was born of a dream to make vacations fun again; to make people forget the time of day and day of week, and to not worry about getting your money's worth or seeing enough sights. The ethos is to explore a few days of connecting with the places you go to and people you meet—as they are; to do things slowly that you have little time for in life; to discover the joys of taking it as it comes and of doing nothing.

Additionally, Vijay has been a data-driven business leader with over twenty years of experience in managing niche businesses globally, using design, innovation and technology. He has won and delivered large and complex deals, turned around troubled relationships, and built and grown presales and delivery organizations. He is passionate about making relationships work, and creating value for his clients, partners and teams.

Chapter 1

Call to Adventure

'Your adventure has to be coming out of your own interior. If you are ready for it, then doors will open where there were no doors before.'

—Joseph Campbell

Most of the entrepreneurs we had a conversation with always talk about the prime point of their adventure, where it all starts. It was this point in time when they were in the idyllic world, complacent in their selves, not feeling the need to do anything different—or maybe they did. Then something happened! The centre of gravity shifted and the hero set off in some direction, often not sure where it would lead.

This starting point is unique for every entrepreneur. While most startup founders try to solve a problem, we stumbled upon many different reasons why people set out on an adventure of entrepreneurship. The reasons could vary from FOMO, the global phenomena of Gen Z, where they feel they are missing out on being in *Forbes* 30 Under 30, or it could be sheer chance, a butterfly effect launching a tornado. It could be dissatisfaction with where they are, a clarion call from one's inner being shouting they can do more, or it could even be an adverse event that could spur them into deliberate action towards a personal journey of evolution.

Whatever the reason, the call to adventure is one step forward despite the weight of inertia, a battle cry to the strong pullback on an individual to stay where he or she is. When someone steps forward despite that inertia, they often set events in motion that could change their lives, as well as those of many others.

> *'Furthermore, we have not even to risk the adventure alone; for the heroes of all time have gone before us; the labyrinth is thoroughly known; we have only to follow the thread of the hero-path.'*
>
> **—Joseph Campbell**

Where's the Blood?

Following the call from within is common among many entrepreneurs we spoke to.

Major Devashish Chakravarty, an Indian Army veteran, has had the journey of a lifetime. Being in the army for almost seventeen years, Devashish was now looking to figure out his new identity. One thing he did know was that he was very good at cracking entrance exams. After his military service, he decided to appear for one of the toughest exams, the Common Admission Test (CAT), where he got a 100 percentile and secured admission in IIM Ahmedabad.

After his first year, Devashish got an internship on Wall Street with one of the biggest investment banks. On the trading floor of Wall Street, he would observe the markets going up and down, and along with it, the emotions of the floor would move from anger to joy to despair to anxiety to relief, every single day. People would be shouting at colleagues, screaming on calls, banging desks, even crying at times. But Devashish did not feel these extreme emotions. He observed that a select few more people on the floor looked completely relaxed, too. He went to one such person:

D: Hey, what happened, why are the people on the floor so angry?

P: The market moved down unexpectedly.

D: But you seem to be not reacting? Are you not trading?

P: I am trading, I don't see any reason to get so emotional.

D: Why do you say so?

P: Where's the blood?

D: Excuse me?

P: Yeah, who's dying? No one. Who's bleeding? No one. What's there to worry about then?

D: Why do you feel that?

P: Because I come from the US Marines.

D: Hey, I am from the Indian Army.

P: (Pointing at other composed traders on the floor): Look at that guy, he is from the Australian defence forces. That one—an Egyptian commando.

In that moment, Devashish understood that on Wall Street, you will either lose or make money on a daily basis. That's all there is to it. A 2 per cent fee will go to the trading firm and 98 per cent to the clients they don't even know. As a trader, if you don't perform well, **the worst case is that**

at the end of the year, you will lose your job—that's about it! Nobody is still going to die or bleed.

This one conversation took away any excitement that Wall Street could offer Devashish. He began seeking the next most exciting thing. What would be as daring as serving in army operations in the Himalayas or fighting battles on high seas? Entrepreneurship was the answer he landed on. That's where our Kargil war veteran hoped to find his identity—but it was the start of a decade-long journey full of unknown challenges.

Exercise

Get connected to your source of inspiration:

1. Find a quiet and comfortable space where you can reflect without distractions. This could be a cozy corner in your home, a serene outdoor spot or any place where you feel at ease.

2. Take a few deep breaths to centre yourself and clear your mind.

3. Close your eyes and visualize the last time you felt truly inspired. Try to recall as many details as possible about the situation. What were you doing? Who were you with? Where were you? What made the experience inspiring?

4. As you remember the experience, pay attention to the emotions it evokes. How did you feel at that moment? What thoughts were running through your mind? Take note of the positive emotions such as excitement, joy or a sense of accomplishment.

5. What's stopping you from feeling that now?

I Just Want to Play Games All Day!

'Entrepreneurship is a tool to achieve my life goals,' says Dharamveer Singh Chouhan, founder of a popular travel startup named Zostel. DV, as he is fondly called, has lived by this statement since he was ten.

As a kid, DV had one dream—to play games all day. Like any other teenager, he continued doing that when he went to middle school. As he got into high school, everyone around him started to ask him his career plans, and he realized he couldn't give silly answers anymore. This is when DV started saying that he will earn money making games. Entrepreneurship became his justification to play games all day, and he started believing in it.

But the journey from here on wasn't as straightforward as he'd imagined. To make a living creating games, he would need to become an engineer. He checked out the top ten colleges in India and set himself a target to get into an IIT. He went to Kota for coaching like thousands of other students. There, he realized that nobody else knows why they want to get into IITs; they were only following the great rat race. The only reason they were slogging is because someone else told them that life would be sorted after getting into an IIT and that was the motivation. There was hardly anyone dreaming of making cars, satellites and rockets. That made him lose interest in going to IITs and he spent his Kota years playing online games and pursuing his passion.

DV appeared in the challenging Joint Entrance Examination for admission into IITs. The top rankers in IIT-JEE typically go to IIT Bombay and most of DV's friends got in. Since he failed to get one of the top ranks, he got into IIT BHU instead. While IIT BHU is a very renowned institution and one of the best in the country, DV was not happy. He missed his friends and felt lonely at a place where a lot of students would feel like they had made it. To distract himself from the loneliness and to deal with the change, he descended into drinking and partying.

DV had a lot of time on campus as his goal was not getting a job or high grades. There was no ticking time bomb in his mind, like a lot of students have. He spent most of his time exploring. The year was 2008, when

Facebook had started emerging. Mark Zuckerberg had become the youngest self-made billionaire at twenty-three. Facebook was becoming a gaming platform on the web, with Zynga making *Mafia Wars* and *Farmville*.

One needs to be honest to oneself in order to improve. DV realized that he was lying to himself that he would get into IIT, become an engineer and then make games. If he wanted to do it, he had to do it now. He embraced the 'first principles method' and approached seniors on how to build games on the web. He learnt Photoshop and web tools and created a fantasy cricket game in 2009. He studied everything on the Internet and taught himself all that he could. He designed the website, learned all the technicalities—front end (HTML, CSS), back end (PHP, MySQL) and hosted it on the cloud. He figured out search engine optimization and calculated the traffic and revenue potential. The work was meticulous. He got traffic on his site, but the site did not make any money. The earnings per click were in cents compared to $6–7 that he had projected. The project was a failure! DV was heartbroken, and it was followed by more months of drinking.

At this stage, DV felt he was missing something and needed guidance. He sought out the best entrepreneurship mind in the country. He went to IIM Ahmedabad for a project under the professor who had made India's first entrepreneurship-cell (E-Cell), Padma Shri Professor Anil Gupta. There he met a startup founder and told him about his failure. The founder motivated him, saying that he was still just twenty years old, the things that he had learned were phenomenal given his age. He should not give up and keep trying. DV once again re-evaluated his position and this conversation accelerated his journey as an entrepreneur.

DV's grandfather is an entrepreneur and his mentor as well. DV once had a conversation with him that changed his perspective.

G: What's going on at IIT?

DV: People are preparing CVs for placements.

G: IITians can have a higher risk appetite. I don't understand that if all of you get into jobs, then who will be creating those jobs?

This made DV emotional towards entrepreneurship, in addition to seeing it as a tool! He decided to keep at it. He created a gaming studio, Bright Ants Gaming Studio, and decided to make games on Facebook. At the studio, he created games like BattleT20, a multiplayer online cricket manager game with over twenty-five event simulations for each ball, as well as iplcricketgame, an online fantasy game. He ran his studio for two years. DV had fulfilled his first goal and was now making a living creating games—for now!

I Was Lost Deep in a Hole

Nihal Ahmed is the founder of Limitless Institute, which helps people discover their purpose. But his own journey started with a profound sense of dissatisfaction. Born into a modest family in India, Nihal was raised with the belief that work was primarily a means to an end—a duty that we do to put food on our tables. You study engineering or become a chartered accountant to build a safety net, and you do this duty as obedient workers. You don't question it or try to understand what all you need to do in your job. Our education system did not give enough room for self-discovery.

It was not much of a surprise then that he ended up pursuing a bachelor's degree in business and finance from a renowned university. He was studying accounting, finance, taxation; destined to be an accountant, destined to work at a bank. He was on a predetermined path to safety, but a nagging feeling persisted. The world of accounting and finance just didn't speak to him!

Nihal wasn't experiencing any joy in his day-to-day life as a college student. He would drag himself to classes and examinations. His first semester grades came in, and they were dismal. He felt like a misfit, a square peg in a round hole. He started hating his life.

Three questions plagued him again and again:

a. What job would really fulfill me?
b. What skills and mindset are needed to be successful in that job?
c. How do I get started?

He tried joining a CA coaching centre to improve his performance. On the first day, he looked at the guy who was teaching. He felt that even the teacher was not doing it out of joy. He was doing it mostly to draw a salary. There was no spark in his eyes. It reminded Nihal once again of the story from his childhood of doing work as a duty. And this was it for Nihal!

He went to the basketball court in his college and sat there for hours, obsessing over the three core questions.

He had been feeling lost in a deep hole for weeks, but now he was determined to break free.

Did You Leave Behind a River in Your Village to Buy a Flat Overlooking a Swimming Pool?

'Who is actually poor? The villager or the urbanite?' asks Mayank Jain, co-founder of SumArth, a startup in the agriculture sector.

Mayank grew up in Delhi as the city was upgrading itself with malls and metros. Everyone in his family had a decent paying job. While growing up, Mayank's plan was to become a consultant for the United Nations and influence policy making.

During the Dussehra of 2014, he got malaria and typhoid at the same time. He was ill from October that year till Diwali in November. This became a period of a lot of self-reflection for him. Like many city dwellers, he was in a demanding corporate job for fifteen hours a day, not paying much heed to anything else. He was not eating well. He was completely disconnected with the food he was consuming, which was low in nutrition. He realized that there was a hidden hunger—lack of nutrients in the food leading to urban populations not having a balanced meal. People were having vegetables not in tune with the seasons and this was leading to chronic health issues.

During his sickness, he started realizing how food affects us. He started learning about the healing powers of nutrients. He started appreciating food once more.

It became clear to him that our food system is broken, and something had to be done. The personal breakdown awakened the entrepreneur in him. He moved to Gaya in Bihar to make food more farm-to-table. He left the malls, metro and friends behind, to a place with not even a single Big Bazaar. He left the comfort of bed to sleep on the floor. He left a comfortable job to grind on the field.

But he also left the polluted air to breathe fresh air. He lost friends but found his community. He eats high-nutrition food today, growing it himself. Not just that— through a network of 25,000 farmers, he is enabling many people to eat healthy. He sleeps peacefully at night while asking himself: Who is actually poor? The villager or the urbanite?

Exercise

The Weekend Hustle: A Self-Discovery Experiment for Aspiring Indian Entrepreneurs

This experiment is designed to help you understand your entrepreneurial spirit and define your personal boundaries for success.

Duration: One weekend (Friday evening to Sunday night)
Materials:

- Journal
- Timer (phone app works)
- List of potential sacrifices (see below)

The Experiment
Day 1: The Allure of the Hustle (Friday evening):

1. **Vision board:** Spend thirty minutes creating a vision board for your entrepreneurial dream. Include images, words and quotes that represent your ideal business and its impact.
2. **The grind:** Set a timer for two hours. During this time, research and write down the key steps needed to launch your business (market research, competitor analysis, financial projections). Imagine yourself fully immersed in the startup process.
3. **Journaling:** Reflect on your experience during the research period. Did you feel energized or

overwhelmed? Jot down any initial doubts or concerns that surfaced.

Day 2: The Sacrifice Spectrum (Saturday):

1. **Potential sacrifices:** Review the list below of common sacrifices entrepreneurs face. Consider the likelihood of facing each one in your specific business venture.

   - **Time:** Reduced personal time, weekends dedicated to work.
   - **Finances:** Limited income during the initial stages, potential personal loans.
   - **Relationships:** Less time for family and friends, potential strain on relationships.
   - **Lifestyle:** Reduced travel, changes in spending habits, potential career breaks.

2. **Sacrifice simulation:** Choose two or three sacrifices from the list that seem most likely for your business. For each sacrifice, dedicate 30 minutes to simulating its impact.

   - **Time:** Set a timer and spend 30 minutes completely disconnected from social media and entertainment, mimicking a busy workday. Reflect on how this feels.

- **Finances:** Create a mock budget assuming a reduced income for a period. Analyse how this might impact your lifestyle.
- **Relationships:** Imagine explaining your potential work schedule to a loved one. Consider how this might affect your relationship.

3. **Journaling:** After each simulation, write down your thoughts and feelings. Did the sacrifice feel manageable? Would it significantly impact your well-being?

Day 3: Defining Your Boundaries (Sunday):

1. **The deal breakers:** Review your journal entries from the previous days. Identify any sacrifices that seem like deal breakers for you. These are your personal boundaries that you wouldn't be willing to cross in pursuit of your dream.

2. **The adjusted vision:** Revisit your vision board. Considering your boundaries, are there any adjustments you need to make to your vision to ensure your well-being?

3. **The commitment:** Write a short statement outlining your commitment to your entrepreneurial

dream. Acknowledge the sacrifices you're willing to make and the boundaries you've defined.

Evaluation:

By the end of the weekend, you'll have a clearer understanding of the sacrifices involved in entrepreneurial dream. You'll have identified your personal boundaries— the point where the cost outweighs the dream. This self-awareness will help you make informed decisions about your entrepreneurial journey.

Additional tips:

- Discuss your experiment with a trusted friend or mentor. Their feedback can provide valuable insights.
- Remember, this is just a starting point. As your business evolves, your sacrifices and boundaries may need to be revisited.

Remember: A successful entrepreneur is not just about ambition, but also about self-awareness and finding the balance between your dreams and your well-being.

I Missed the Bus

'The cave you fear to enter holds the treasure you seek. Fear of the unknown is our greatest fear.'
                                              —Joseph Campbell

For a satellite to leave Earth, it needs the initial escape velocity. For many entrepreneurs, that 'escape velocity' is a 'life event' that wakes them from their slumber. One such story is that of Phanindra Sama.

'I was an accidental entrepreneur,' says Phanindra, founder of redBus, a travel startup that was destined to reach epic milestones. Born in Nizamabad, Andhra Pradesh, Phani (as he is normally referred to) was always a bright star in academics. He was a state ranker in school and distinction holder from BITS Pilani. He was well-respected in his family circles, and everyone knew he would achieve something great one day. His schoolteacher challenged him to get a district rank and his principal a state rank. He set for himself a dream of making a microchip in one year that he could carry in his wallet, which landed him the highest campus package among his friends when he joined the prestigious BITS Pilani. He kept moving from one orbit to the next. As he kept achieving more things, it kept adding to his self-confidence.

And one day, he missed his bus. Phani was planning to go for a Diwali vacation to his hometown. He says, 'In 2005, the bus system was quite fragmented and run by private operators. Most of them are very small time, owning two or four buses. These operators assign agents across the town. People have to go to the agents to buy tickets. Whenever a customer comes, the agent picks up the phone and asks the operator if there are any seats on that route. Every bus operator maintains one book for each bus. Each book will have thirty pages for each day of the month, and each page would have fifty boxes. Each box represents a seat. If you ask for a ticket for 15 October, then they will go to the fifteenth page and see which of the boxes are empty. That's how a ticket gets booked. During Diwali of 2005, Phani's agent called four or five bus operators, who mentioned that there were no seats available. He went to a few more agents but couldn't secure a ticket. Finally, he had to spend his Diwali in Bengaluru, away from home.

This kept Phani awake all night. The next morning, he discovered that there are at least thirty bus operators between Bengaluru and Hyderabad. The agents could not cover all the operators manually. The system was not efficient, and information wasn't seamlessly available. Agents were making random calls depending on a guess of who would have the inventory. The customer was left without a seat and the bus operator had to go with a vacant seat while paying the same for fuel. This was a problem for all the parties but also an opportunity.

By then, having passed out of BITS Pilani, Phani had become super confident as a person, and believed he could solve big problems. Interestingly, Phani didn't think of the opportunity as a startup. He decided to create an open source software to solve the problem. He wanted to give the bus operators the software that would give him access to the bus inventory, which could be then used for booking by the agents. He was trying to create a solution from what he knew—he just wanted to solve the problem.

He did not want anyone else to miss the bus like he did. He had many more challenges while building it out, but he could always go back to his call to adventure—**a personal moment where something failed.**

That moment where you realize that something is missing and going forth to find it defines an entrepreneur. All entrepreneurs that we spoke to always had a gleam of hope in their eyes when they spoke about the initial call to adventure. With a small smile, they recount how a journey of a thousand miles started.

Doodling Your Future to Life

Alicia Souza is an innovative and trailblazing illustrator renowned for her relatable and captivating illustrations. Over the last seven years, she quickly garnered a large following due to her charming depictions of everyday moments and emotions, often featuring endearing characters accompanied by witty captions. Her work can be found across a variety of mediums, including stationery, home decor and digital content. With a strong presence on social media platforms like Instagram, where her audience exceeds half a million followers, Souza shares her delightful illustrations and engages with her fans with an authenticity that endears her. Additionally, she has launched her own line of products, from greeting cards to notebooks to planners, all adorned with her unique artwork.

Born and raised in Abu Dhabi, Alicia showed early signs of diligence and determination as a student. Whenever she came across a drawing, she would fixate on it with unwavering focus, trying to decipher its secrets. To her, drawing was like a puzzle waiting to be solved. With her exceptional work ethic, she not only mastered the art of drawing but also developed her own signature style. Her passion led her to Melbourne to pursue communication design in college. There, she was exposed to various fields that ignited possibilities for post-graduation endeavours.

While many graduates aimed for roles in design or art direction, Alicia remained steadfast in her desire to focus solely on her craft, which is drawing, rather than managing other people who would bring it to life. Many creatives who get into the field always face this Catch-22 situation—the dilemma between pursuing art purely for art's sake so that they can nurture personal expression versus for practical application. The market typically has more roles to scale a craft rather than people who can ideate and create the craft. Alicia's soul burns with unbridled passion for her craft—illustration. This North Star guided Alicia throughout her career, where no matter what happened, she stayed on course for what she considered was her true calling.

After graduating, Alicia tried her hand at various jobs: working in a cafe, then at a bank. But she always had a burning desire to create something of her own. That's when she co-founded Chumbak, a design-led retail brand, and moved to Bengaluru, India. However, things didn't go as planned and Alicia had to exit Chumbak. She suddenly found herself starting over in a new country with only five acquaintances and little money. Faced with this uncertainty, she knew she had to hustle to make her dreams a reality. She began searching for freelance work, but it was tough. She would meet potential clients and pitch her ideas. Often, they were unsure of what they wanted or if they could afford her services. On top of that, there wasn't much demand for illustrations in the country and her talent wasn't fully appreciated. The journey had been tough for her, wrought with obstacles and doubts. But Alicia held onto hope that in Bengaluru, she could still build a successful and fulfilling career.

Bengaluru, the garden city of endless possibilities, hosts an event called Sunday Soul Sante, where visual artists and performers showcase their talents. Alicia, determined to make a name for herself in the world of illustration, took a chance and exhibited some of her products there. While she was nervous at the outset, she wanted to explore what she could do. Her work was received positively and was a roaring success as all her merchandise sold out. She felt like this could be her big break. However, she could not find the right business partner, leaving her to handle all the logistics and management on her own while juggling her freelance work.

From timid beginnings and being an introvert, hesitant to share her work on social media, Alicia pushed through with unwavering focus because she knows that success takes hard work. Despite her undeniable talent in drawing, Alicia never rested on her laurels—for success is a constant battle to better oneself. It's not just about meeting the expectations of the world, but also constantly pushing oneself to surpass them. For Alicia, success means enduring an endless cycle of receiving briefs, creating sketches and anxiously waiting for client approval. While the world might see only the romantic version of the job, there is a lot of hard work behind it.

To some, drawing may seem like a simple job, but Alicia knows the harsh reality of pouring blood, sweat and tears into making a living as an artist. And yet for her, it's all worth it for the chance to turn something ordinary into pure magic through hard work and unwavering determination. The world of creativity is a constantly shifting and unpredictable one. The preferences and tastes of target audiences can change at any moment, while corporate budgets may suddenly shrink. This reality requires a constant state of hard work and adaptability for creative entrepreneurs. It may serve as a harsh dose of reality for those who aspire to be in these positions, but the truth is that success in this field is earned through relentless effort and ingenuity.

Another year went by and Alicia now had become a known name with many firms in Bengaluru for her work. She had enough freelancing projects to bring her attention back to what she had always wanted to do—have a product in her name! She crossed paths with Saurabh Sharma, who offered her a chance to partner with him, where he would manufacture, and she could do what she was good at—draw. This was ideal as it would give her time to create and not focus on other areas. What started as a small pilot for two months has now turned into seven years of immense success, making 'Alicia Souza' one of the top brands in the illustrations and design spaces. She churns out products like photo albums, stationery, journals, stamps, gift boxes and has a loyal fan base that is growing and looks forward to her products. As an entrepreneur, Alicia looks back and smiles, fondly sharing how everything happens for a reason. She has transformed obstacles into opportunities as they have appeared and has been able to strike the right balance between her vocation and passion.

Every year, she ships out a yearly planner, which gets sold out quickly. In this planner, one of the elements is a letter that one writes to oneself a year down the line to open 365 days later.

Exercise

Here is an activity for you in the same spirit. Write a letter to the future entrepreneur, which is YOU, three years later:

<To be opened three years from <today's date>>
Dear <your name>,

Yours sincerely,

What's My Tribe?

The Oxford English Dictionary meaning of the word 'deliberate' is 'to consider something very carefully, usually before making a decision'. We are deliberate about so many things in our life—jobs, friends, toothpaste! But one thing people in India are not deliberate about and take for granted is the community they are a part of. We are born into a part of the country that has a specific culture, and the value system is often designed to keep you rooted to it, whether your calling aligns to it or not.

Mayur Sontakke is from Kolhapur, Maharashtra, where he grew up in a joint family. At a very young age, he wanted to see the world and make a dent. However, his exposure was limited, and opportunities were within a certain sphere only as he tried to break through. He started a merchandise business followed by a language learning startup, trying to make that dent to find his space in the sun. However, this was pre-2010; the Internet and digital domain had not yet picked up across the country, leave alone suburban Maharashtra. Realizing that the business is not scalable or viable, our seeker decided to refuse the call of entrepreneurship and joined a financial credit rating firm. He worked there from 2010 to 2014, building his skill set in the corporate world but always hoping that one day, he would get an opportunity to do something different, to find his calling.

In 2014, Mayur got an opportunity to work in a role that was remote. He started working from home but then slowly realized that this was his cue to experiment, an opportunity to spread his wings. He had a friend in Trichy, Tamil Nadu, with whom he decided to go to Varkala, a coastal town in the southern part of Kerala known for its cliffs overlooking beaches. He arrived there and started working while using his free time to explore the pristine nature of the coastal town. He loved the opportunity to be closer to nature while contributing to work.

Given that he had just started working remotely, he wanted to experiment to see if it was possible to be productive while working from a place away from the office. A month converted into two months and then three by the beach. Next, Mayur decided to level up and moved to the mountains. He travelled to Himachal for three months and from there on, kept moving! He realized he can be productive and work from anywhere, asking himself questions that were only so far deep within him— what is the purpose of technology? Is it for people to be hooked to screens or lead better lives consciously? Am I spending time with people I want to be with?

As he observed his peers, who were all getting married and starting families, he came to the realization that he did not want that—yet. He needed to be close to the 'community' he found while he was travelling— adventurous, entrepreneurial, growth-minded people with whom he could learn and evolve and finally discover his calling. He wondered if there was a gap in the market where he saw people save up money to travel and be with communities of like-minded people only to go back to unsustainable cities, getting stuck in traffic and waiting for the next trip to be themselves again.

The next adventure took Mayur to Southeast Asia for a workation of eight months, where he backpacked across Thailand, Indonesia, Cambodia, Malaysia and Vietnam. He was exposed to communities of global digital nomads who lived and worked in like-minded communities. During this period, he met his biggest cheerleader and support system, his wife, Joy. They travelled together and Mayur realized what his calling really was—to be productive, close to nature and to grow with a community.

Joy helped Mayur organize his thoughts, crowdsource and set up NomadGao, a digital nomad community. They quickly set up centres in Goa and Himachal Pradesh. The seeker from Kolhapur travelled the world to give back and enable professionals to work from anywhere. Imagine working virtually through the day to closing your laptop and the workspace being cleared for an open mic—there would be poetry, theatre and singing—all next to nature and amidst people who understand you. Would that make you more productive? Would that help entrepreneurs come together for fresh ideas? These are answers awaiting you when you try out the life of a digital nomad.

For Mayur, he went on to work with the Goa government to make Goa popular among digital nomads and work on building further communities. His attempt to bring conscious living and authentic human connections was a call to adventure that he set out on from Kolhapur, and he's on the path to learning and growing his tribe every day.

Each entrepreneur has a unique reason for starting up. It could range from following the wolf call from within, like DV, or wanting to make an impact for the better, like Mayank. While you could be looking to solve a problem like Phani, you could also be trying to find your tribe like Mayur. As you take inspiration from these stories, you should understand that there is no set path and once you are awake to your being and mission, the destiny of being an entrepreneur will find you in myriad ways.

What we have found common in many stories is the theme of an individual deciding to own his or her story. After being tossed around by the waves, a determined entrepreneur wakes up to the realization that the journey must start. The journey ahead is shrouded in mist and while they do not know what it will bring, they know that the time to try is now.

> *'The big question is whether you are going to be able to say a hearty yes to your adventure.'*
> —**Joseph Campbell**

Exercise

Think of the entrepreneur you want to be. Envision it. What did they do? What would they do if they were in your position now? Track your choices over time.

Chapter 2

Refusal of the Call

'The myths and folktales of the whole world make it clear that the refusal is essentially a refusal to give up what one takes to be one's own interest.'
—**Joseph Campbell**[1]

What is perceived today, but is far from the truth, is that once an entrepreneur sets out on their call to adventure, the next step is overnight success. In our culture of instant gratification, the celebration of success overtakes the various twists and turns of the journey. It is seen that in many instances, after an entrepreneur has determined to start the journey, fear takes centre stage and asks debilitating questions of the aspiring entrepreneur: Are you sure you

---

[1] Joseph Campbell, *The Hero with a Thousand Faces* (Princeton, NJ: Princeton University Press, 1949), 59.

want to do this? Are you good enough or an imposter? What if you fail?

India post-1991 has been the famed land of opportunities. Economic growth has brought with it a growing Indian middle class that has aspirations and dreams to conquer the world, but also the dreaded fear: 'What if you fail?' Gen X has grown up in a transition from License Raj to Instagram. Hence, when their children go out to raise funding or buy office space, it is only obvious that parents raise the question of a parachute, safety and stability—valid concerns from their perspective. The parents grew up in a time when a government or salaried job was the epitome of success and risk-taking ability was seen as foolhardiness. The fear somehow comes handed down as legacy to the next generation and often leads to entrepreneurs stepping away from the adventure—in doubt.

Pre-1991, in a traditional business setup, culturally youngsters did not have much of a career choice. It was assumed that they would continue the family business or whatever path their parents set out for them. With the emergence of education as a core value, things started to change. India started to produce a record number of middle-class engineers. As the joke goes, 'You do

engineering and then decide what you want to do with life.'
Now, they have a choice—to take up a secure job OR to
be in business.

And it's difficult to make this choice. For someone who
has business running in their DNA, it can become suffocating
to be in a job for long. But then it's a big opportunity cost to
let go of a lifestyle that every middle-class family aspires for.
An engineer in a job with a decade worth of work experience
can help clear up family loans, build a house for parents,
etc. This is huge—even if it wouldn't lead to a heavy bank
balance at any moment of time, it helps in cutting down
costs significantly.

With this education, it's difficult to get back to family
business as well. A software engineer sitting at a kirana
store seems out of place.

So, what do you do? How do you make the choice?

The Fear Is Real

Devashish Chakravarty had his call to adventure for
entrepreneurship. But he only experienced one emotion
while starting up—**pure fear!**

Once, he went for a solo skydiving course in South
Africa. He had to sit inside a small plane with his
belongings. They provided training for a day, so you could

know everything that you needed to. There was a small doorway in the plane, three feet by two feet. Close to ten people were cramped in the small plane waiting for their turn to jump. When your time came, you had to go out of the doorway and climb out on the wing of the aircraft. It's a standard wing, which had rods underneath. The rods were connected to the wing and supported it. You are supposed to go out on the wing holding the rod. If you directly jumped, you might hit the tail of the aircraft, so you are required to walk a bit on the wing. And then let go with your hands and feet.

Devashish observed a couple of people jump ahead of him, and the instructor told him to go out on the wing. The problem was that he wasn't able to move. He felt something was holding onto his legs, folded behind him. The instructor saw him and responded that there was nothing. Devashish felt that it might be a cramp in that case. His legs had become like dead weight. His mind was playing such huge tricks that he was paralyzed from the waist downwards. His legs were not listening to him. They were least interested in going out. Finally, the instructor lifted one leg and put it outside. Devashish now put both his hands on the rod. His other leg and body were still inside. The instructor then lifted the other leg and put it outside. Now, both of Devashish's legs were stuck to the wing and ready to let go. Meanwhile, his hands were turning white in the cold wind that was blowing at 180 kmph, to which he was not oblivious. His body was in full survival mode and completely seizing up. He also experienced a sense of guilt that he was taking more time than required and others were waiting in queue. Time was standing still for him. The instructor encouraged him to let go. Devashish's army training subconsciously kicked in to follow orders. And so, he let go of his hands and his body followed for his first solo jump.

Devashish recalls that this was the kind of fear he experienced when he was committing to entrepreneurship. When he was signing the document, giving away his pre-placement offer and job, he felt a paralysing fear. He realized that he was used to the government job and the four decades of pay security that came with it. Compared to that, he now had zero visibility and didn't know what was going to happen the next day.

Devashish realized that if he was asked to be James Bond, drive the plane solo and jump, he would never have been able to do so. It was only because of the instructor and other divers who were really calm around him that he could do it. At a later stage, our army major found calm in the courage of his younger co-founders to overcome the refusal of the call.

Exercise: Identifying Your Fears:

- **What specifically am I afraid of when it comes to starting my business?** (Fear of failure, financial insecurity, market uncertainty, etc.)
- **How realistic are these fears?** (Research market trends, talk to entrepreneurs in your field to assess actual risks.)
- **How would these fears potentially impact my decision-making?** (Would they lead to inaction or overly cautious choices?)

Understanding Your Tolerance for Risk:

- **How comfortable am I with taking calculated risks?** (Analyze past situations where you faced uncertainty.)
- **What is my worst-case scenario, and how would I handle it?** (Plan for potential setbacks.)
- **What is my risk tolerance compared to other successful entrepreneurs?** (Research the journeys of others in your field.)

Building Confidence and Overcoming Fear:

- **What skills and knowledge do I currently possess that can help me succeed?** (Focus on your strengths.)
- **What knowledge gaps do I have, and how can I address them?** (Create a learning plan.)
- **What small, achievable milestones can I set to build my confidence?** (Celebrating early wins can boost your belief in yourself.)
- **What strategies have other entrepreneurs used to overcome similar fears?** (Learn from their experiences.)
- **Can I reframe my fear as a motivating force that pushes me to be more prepared?** (View fear as a signal to be cautious and plan effectively.)

Developing a Support System:

- **Who can I talk to about my fears and anxieties?** (Mentors, peers, family or a therapist.)
- **Can I find a community of aspiring entrepreneurs for support and shared experiences?** (Look for online forums or local groups.)

By asking yourself these questions, you can gain a deeper understanding of your fear of the unknown and develop a personalized plan to address it. Remember, most successful entrepreneurs experience fear, but they learn to manage it and take action despite the uncertainty.

Self-Doubt Is Viral

While building software, we often look at funnels for observations. How many new customers downloaded the app, how many added a product to the cart, and how many people made the payment. By observing these funnels, we can identify what most of the users are doing. What per cent is simply downloading and forgetting about the app, compared to the per cent of actual buyers. Similarly, if we look at the funnel of entrepreneurship, sadly 90 per cent of people will fall even before the phase of their call to adventure. You can find examples all around you. In fact, all of us at some point in time have faced this as well. The challenge is that many are not even aware of the call to adventure. Our middle-class machine is designed to maximize stability. For that, the formula is to study hard, get into IITs and get a job in an MNC. The fear of failing is so high that no one in my childhood came and told me to 'dream' or to 'discover yourself'. The path was predefined. And this can have a huge impact.

Samarth Mahajan is a national award-winning filmmaker today. But ten years ago, he was at his lowest point of mental health. His is a story of how the rat race is so ingrained in us that it can make us devoid of any other thought.

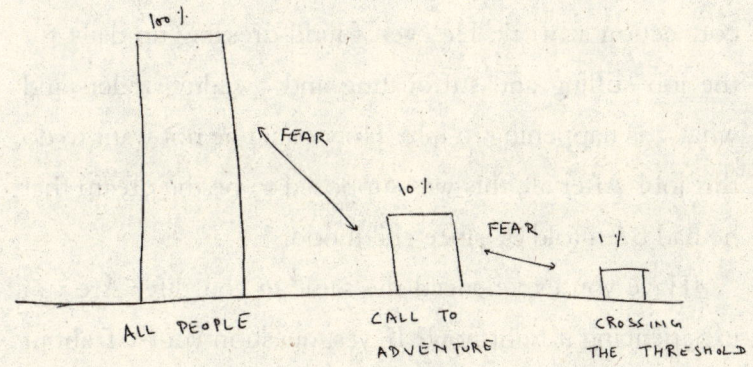

Samarth was born in a small border village of Punjab, where he spent nineteen years of his life. He studied hard and secured admission in IIT Kharagpur. His only goal for the next four years was to get a day-one placement. He was told that his life would be sorted after that. For twenty-three years of his life, Samarth only worked towards building his resume. There was no other hobby and no other purpose. He joined the robotics club in college and got good grades, all so that he could get the 'dream job'. Our society structure is such that we never pause to question: Is 'the' dream job 'my' dream job as well?

Within one year of his job, Samarth started feeling out of place. He was in his favourite city—Kolkata—but when the mind is restless, even the best of surroundings can't rescue us. He was feeling dissatisfied and lacking any connection at work. He even found dressing up daily for the job stifling and suffocating and couldn't understand what was happening to him. How could he not want to do this job? After all, this was supposed to be the dream that he had been told of since childhood.

Have you experienced the same in your life? Are you experiencing it right now? If yes, question yourself about whether you are walking in someone else's footsteps. Maybe your destiny lies towards the right of the funnel.

EMI of Opportunity Cost

Getting back to our redBus founder, Phani realized there was a problem to be solved, and it had potential. But he knew he could not do it alone. So, he wrote to the group of people he knew best—his seven college flatmates, with whom he shared a close bond. He explained the problem of how the bus system was not efficient, that bus operators were manually using a network to fill seats and how there was a big gap in demand and supply, because of which our entrepreneur famously missed his bus. The seven friends started to work on bringing something new to the world.

However, it was a bumpy bus ride on a rural road from there on. Given the costs of building a website and low commissions, Phani and his co-founders struggled to make even a few thousand rupees a week, even after a few months. Doubts started creeping in if they were on the right track. Leaving plush jobs to try entrepreneurship is never easy. You face your own demons at every step. Phani, at this stage, did not know if his idea was viable and if he was leading his friends on a wild goose chase.

Add to that the feedback from professors and ex-colleagues, who perceived bus agencies as the mafia and illegal. A BITS Pilani graduate could do anything but drop a conventional, well-paying job! This was a time when Phani thought he should quit, refuse this call to adventure and get back to the beaten path that offered predictability and safety.

Fear of failure and the opportunity cost of not pursuing the path is a deadly combination, like stone fetters for any budding entrepreneur.

So, how do entrepreneurs overcome their fears? Let's find out!

Plan Your Act and Act Your Plan

How do you overcome fear? How do you face doubt and darkness in your soul that is not rational? The answer lies in realizing that entrepreneurship is a marathon, not a sprint. Your journey as an entrepreneur can start way earlier than when your company gets registered.

Ankit Jain, co-founder of GDi Partners, sets a great example of how to go about it. Coming from a humble background in a small town called Ghatshila in Jharkhand, Ankit somewhere always knew he wanted to challenge the status quo and be a social entrepreneur someday. He found himself drawn to taking new initiatives and joined college societies and clubs that were focused on social impact, as well as organizations in their nascent stages.

This is what led Ankit to embrace a savings mindset throughout his college. He resisted the temptation to splurge—to the extent that he did not even go to a nearby beach trip for the four years of college, where almost 99 per cent of the campus went. Post-college, Ankit took a secure job with an MNC based out of a tier-2 city. Over the next three years, he cleared his education loan and got a house built for his family in Ghatshila, where his family could live comfortably. This is when Ankit decided to switch domains and start doing what he loved. He got into the social impact sector after taking a huge pay cut.

Still, he knew he couldn't jump into starting a business anytime soon. Over the next five years, while learning about the social sector, he gradually got to a zone of financial safety—a financial position to sustain himself and family for a couple of years. Now, with the acquired knowledge and capital safety, he decided to start his business. This is a perfect example of how the entrepreneur needs to plan one's act and act one's plan while running the marathon of entrepreneurship.

It is easier to cross the stage of 'refusal of the call' if you 'plan your act and act your plan'.

It is evident what keeps people from planning, acting and starting up is the fear of change. In her research, Dr Elisabeth Kübler-Ross connects the fear of change to the stages of dying.[2] There is shock, denial, anger and acceptance as one goes through a change in the status quo. The journey of entrepreneurship could be about

---

[2] Elisabeth Kübler-Ross, *On Death and Dying* (New York: Macmillan, 1969)

the fear of failure but also the fear of success—basically a subconscious intent to not change things based on the fear of 'what if it gets worse'. The weight of the unknown turns into fetters on ankles and keeps you from moving forward resolutely.

> 'Often in actual life, and not infrequently in the myths and popular tales, we encounter the dull case of the call unanswered; for it is always possible to turn the ear to other interests. Walled in boredom, hard work, or "culture", the subject loses the power of significant affirmative action and becomes a victim to be saved.'
>
> —**Joseph Campbell**

Master Your Craft

> 'If you are given to run the Times of India (TOI) and you do not know your subject, TOI might not survive. But if you are given only Rs 10,000 and you know your subject, you can do wonders with it!'
>
> —*Sangeeta Saxena, renowned defence journalist*

Sangeeta Saxena is the founder of a defence news portal, named Aviation and Defence Universe (ADU). She has been a renowned defence journalist for past three decades. Sangeeta got married at the age of twenty and raised two children, who are well settled. Life was passing by smoothly between fulfilling the roles of an army wife, mother of two kids and a professional journalist.

She was working with a well-respected magazine for defence and aerospace. Being a senior journalist, she used to cover interviews with industry CEOs. They had a magazine of eighty-two pages, four of which went in front and back covers. There was a page for the table of contents and the editorial. Advertisers took away another ten pages. Then, there were regulars, leaving limited space for special coverages. Sangeeta feared that if her interviews did not get published, her reputation in the industry would get tarnished. That happened twice in 2014. In 2015, she did an interview with the leader of one of the biggest aerospace companies in the world, but the editorial committee informed her that its publishing would need to be postponed due to paucity of space. This made her furious. Sangeeta decided at that moment that she did not want to work like this anymore!

Sangeeta resigned and informed everyone that she wouldn't be coming from the next day. The very same day, she decided to start her own magazine. She was an expert in her subject of defence journalism, but there were many challenges ahead. For example:

- Publishing every print edition comes with an expense of Rs 5 lakh, and she did not have this money.
- The new-age medium is digital, not print. She had no exposure to running a website.
- She had just one month to launch the website, as she had declared that the best day to launch for an aerospace journalist would be the Indian Air Force Day. The team had no time to do test runs.
- She did not know what Search Engine Optimisation (SEO) is.
- Everyone in the family was in the services, hence sceptical of running a business.
- She did not know marketing, and only two out of ten clients would respond.
- Women journalists are taken very sceptically in the field of aerospace and defence in India. She realized that she would have to prove herself continuously.
- She had an intermittent break from mainstream media in various phases of her career.

Naturally, Sangeeta was consumed by fear and doubts. So, how did she overcome the fear and keep moving forward?

By knowing her subject and playing to her strengths!
Sangeeta says that as long as she was providing great
content, she knew she would be okay. She was an expert
already and kept adding to her professional knowledge
bank every day.

As entrepreneurs, there will be many challenges for
which nobody prepares you. Those are the moments when
you doubt yourself the most. Those are the moments when
you feel a refusal of your call to adventure and just want to
turn back to comfort. Those are the moments of fear. If
you know your subject deeply, it will become a great tool
for you to be able to move ahead. In technical terms, this
is what is referred to as the 'founder-market fit'.

The journey of entrepreneurship is not a straight
line. It is not a bunch of tips that can be collated from
the entrepreneurs we spoke to. It is a collection of many
experiences, especially times when we are assailed by
doubts and pulled back by many factors, including fear and
self-doubt. The fear and the inertia are real and debilitating.
The first step towards understanding this stage in an
entrepreneur's journey is identifying it. Once you know
what you fear, uncertainty recedes, and you are ready to
challenge it head-on.

Exercise

Ask yourself: 'What am I most afraid about if I want to be an entrepreneur?' Answer the question. With each answer, take a breath and notice what's happening in your body. Then ask yourself: 'And then what?' Keep asking, 'And then what', with breaths and body awareness in between each. Do this until you get to what's at the core of your fear. You may find that it's not what you thought it was!

Chapter 3

Mentor's Aid

'People say that what we're all seeking is a meaning for life. I don't think that's what we're really seeking. I think that what we're seeking is an experience of being alive.'

—Joseph Campbell

Entrepreneurship is one way to pursue this experience of aliveness. It is a journey into the unknown, where you must face your fears, overcome your challenges and create something new and valuable. It is not an easy path, and it can be lonely and dark at times. You may feel like you are surrounded by dangers and uncertainties, and that you have no one to guide you or support you. You may doubt yourself and your abilities and wonder if you are on the right track.

Imagine a young entrepreneur standing at the edge of a bustling city, where the skyline stretches far into the horizon. The streets are filled with opportunity, but they are also tangled, confusing and chaotic. Without a North Star, this entrepreneur is like a lone traveller with no map. He has ideas and energy but no clear path to follow.

He takes one street, hoping it leads to success, only to find it stops at a dead end—wasting time, money and effort. As he backtracks, his confidence wanes and self-doubt creeps in. Around him, he sees other entrepreneurs moving quickly, seemingly knowing exactly where they're headed, guided by unseen hands, while he struggles to make sense of the maze.

The entrepreneur tries to build relationships but feels unsure of how to approach investors or collaborators. Opportunities slip through his fingers because he lacks the knowledge and connections that could have been handed to him by someone more experienced. He works tirelessly but feels as if he's running in circles, exhausted yet no closer to his goals.

Without someone to show him shortcuts or warn him of pitfalls, he stumbles repeatedly. His vision remains hazy because no one is there to help sharpen it, and the confidence that once fuelled his journey fades with each misstep. Alone in this bustling city of entrepreneurship, he feels isolated and overwhelmed—he struggles to find his way.

But he need not be alone. In many heroes' journeys, there is a moment when the hero meets a mentor, someone who has been there before, who knows the way and who can offer wisdom and assistance. The mentor is a manifestation of your destiny, a sign that you are meant to follow this path and that you have the potential to succeed. This mentor helps you overcome your fears, teaches you new skills and connects you with valuable resources. The mentor shows you that you are not just an ordinary person, but a chosen one, with a special mission and a unique gift.

Many entrepreneurs are hesitant to admit when they are struggling emotionally or when their businesses are not performing as expected, fearing that it will make them look weak or incompetent. Mentors offer a safe space where entrepreneurs can be open about their fears, insecurities and mental health struggles without judgement. This can be crucial in fostering emotional well-being and allowing entrepreneurs to feel comfortable asking for help when needed.

In current times, Indian entrepreneurs, especially women and those from marginalized communities, often face additional emotional burdens linked to societal expectations. Gender roles, family responsibilities and societal stereotypes can create pressure, doubly so in conservative settings. A mentor, who has overcome similar barriers, can provide not only tactical advice but also emotional strength and inspiration, empowering entrepreneurs to push through cultural and societal challenges. Imagine being in the same room as Kiran Mazumdar-Shaw or Indra Nooyi and learning from their experiences.

The connection between traditional entrepreneur mentorship and the **guru-shishya** tradition in India is deeply rooted in the country's cultural heritage. The guru-shishya tradition, which emphasizes a mentor-disciple relationship, has long been a cornerstone of knowledge transfer in various fields, including arts, sciences and philosophy. Similarly, in entrepreneurship, mentors play a crucial role in guiding aspiring business leaders through the complexities of starting and running a venture.

In the guru-shishya framework, the guru (mentor) imparts wisdom, skills and values to the shishya (disciple), fostering a holistic learning environment. This relationship is built on trust, respect and a commitment to personal growth. In the realm of entrepreneurship, mentors serve as guides who share their experiences, offer strategic advice and instill a sense of accountability, much like the guru. They provide not only technical knowledge but also insights into navigating challenges, making ethical decisions and developing resilience.

Moreover, both traditions emphasize the importance of lifelong learning and adaptability. Just as shishyas are encouraged to evolve and question their understanding, entrepreneurs are urged to remain open to feedback and innovation. The guru-shishya tradition, with its focus on mentorship, has influenced modern entrepreneurial practices in India, highlighting the timeless value of guidance, knowledge sharing and personal development in achieving success.

Mentors can also be powerful catalysts for networking opportunities in entrepreneurship by opening doors that might otherwise remain closed. Here's how they provide networking advantages:

1. **Access to Established Networks**

   Mentors often have years of experience and have built extensive personal and professional networks. They can introduce an entrepreneur to key players—whether that's investors, potential business partners, clients or industry experts.

Instead of cold outreach, the entrepreneur can gain immediate trust through their mentor's warm introductions. For example, a mentor who has worked in venture capital might introduce an entrepreneur to a group of investors, accelerating the funding process.

2. **Leveraging Credibility**

Entrepreneurs, especially when starting out, may struggle with credibility. When a mentor vouches for their mentee, it lends credibility to the entrepreneur's ideas, giving them a stronger chance of being heard and taken seriously. For example, in a competitive pitch scenario, an entrepreneur backed by a respected mentor is more likely to get noticed because they come with a stamp of approval from someone already established in the field.

3. **Refining the Entrepreneur's Networking Approach**

Beyond direct introductions, mentors teach entrepreneurs how to effectively network. This involves coaching them on how to build relationships, follow up, present themselves professionally and make lasting impressions. For instance, a mentor can help an entrepreneur refine their elevator pitch, ensuring they communicate their business idea clearly and concisely when meeting potential partners or investors.

We have seen the role of mentors in many stories. Take the example of Po from *Kung Fu Panda*. He was a fan of kung fu, but he had no idea how to learn it or practice it. He knew he needed a teacher, someone who could show him the secrets of this ancient art. He was lucky enough to meet Master Shifu, who recognized his potential and trained him according to his strengths and motivations (food!). Shifu taught Po the skills and techniques that enabled him to defeat the formidable Tai Lung.

As you embark on your entrepreneurial journey, you may also encounter mentors who can help you along the way. They may be people you admire or respect, people who have achieved what you aspire to achieve or people who share your vision or values. They may be formal or informal mentors, paid or unpaid mentors, long-term or short-term mentors. They may be found in various places, such as online platforms, networking events, incubators, accelerators or educational programmes. The important thing is to seek them out, listen to them, learn from them and appreciate them.

A Mentor Sees Past You

After passing out from BITS Pilani, Phani got his dream job, as planned. He wanted to make a microchip that fit into a wallet and that finally took him to Texas Instruments in Bengaluru. While he was working at TI, he missed his bus.

As he set about solving the bus problem, he realized that he needed someone to guide him to build a business. While he did have an idea, he did not yet know the path on what to do next. Doubts often plague entrepreneurs as they move from idea to execution, stemming from uncertainties about market demand, competition or their own capabilities. In the early stages, they may question whether their idea is innovative enough or if it solves a real problem. Fear of failure, along with external pressures, can lead to hesitation or second-guessing decisions. This internal battle can create a cycle of indecision, making it difficult to maintain confidence and momentum throughout the entrepreneurial journey.

Being in a new city where he did not have networks yet and was still battling questions, Phani realized that he had to reach out to learn. He researched, discovered and joined TiE – The Indus Entrepreneurs. TiE is a networking organization that believes in the power of ideas to change the face of entrepreneurship and growing business through five pillars—mentoring, networking, education, incubating and funding. Phani was in an Entrepreneurship Acceleration Programme and got connected with Sanjay Anandaram, an IIM Bangalore alumnus who has spent his life advising startups.

The interesting thing about a mentor is that they will often see things you might miss. Sanjay listened to Phani's open source approach with great interest but also saw something bigger, something Phani had yet to realize. He believed that Phani was sitting on an opportunity to build a **transformative business**, not just a technology solution. He encouraged Phani to think beyond the engineer's perspective and look at the problem as a potential entrepreneur. During one pivotal conversation, Sanjay explained that while the open source idea was noble, it would be limited in its impact unless there was a clear business model to support its growth. He said, 'If you want to create real change, especially in a fragmented industry like bus transportation, you need to build a scalable platform that can bring all stakeholders together in one place—bus operators, travellers and agents.

That won't happen through an open source tool. It will require a business with dedicated resources and a clear vision for the future.'

Sanjay advised Phani that redBus shouldn't just be an open source idea. It was an investable business that had the potential to grow. Without Sanjay's advice, redBus would be one of the fun ideas you discussed with friends but never did anything about. That is the power of mentorship. Not just building a network, but being a part of it and surrounding yourself with it increases the possibilities of people and ideas colliding—and that is where the magic lies.

Design Your Inspiration

Nihal was now desperate to find answers to his three core questions:

a. What job would really fulfil me?
b. What skills and mindset are needed to be successful in that job?
c. How do I get started?

Nihal believes that in India, we don't really have a culture of mentors. While role models like 'tauji', a family member who built a successful business from scratch, were plentiful, true mentors were hard to find. Most of the time, we don't even realize that we need one.

One day, Nihal shared his worries with a friend. And that changed everything. His friend informed him about someone who was leading a student movement. The leader used to collect insights with people from Ivy League institutions and then teach these to volunteers in India. They would then go and teach at universities and low-income schools.

His friend encouraged Nihal to participate. Nihal had his doubts, but he decided to trust his friend's judgement. Within a few weeks, he was blown away. The experience had opened him up to a whole new world—the exciting field of social entrepreneurship.

The leader became a close collaborator with Nihal and shaped a lot of his thinking. Nihal took him on as a mentor and started learning design thinking and frameworks to solve complex human problems. These tools helped Nihal ask more specific questions, such as:

a. What do I love so much that when I am engaged in it, I lose track of time?
b. What am I so good at that people, when they see me, immediately attach that attribute to me?

These questions led to a breakthrough. Nihal started to see a clearer picture of his passions, skills and aspirations. The answers to his three core questions began to emerge. Once that happened, many possibilities started to emerge for Nihal.

A lot of his friends were also craving answers for the same core questions. As Nihal's self-awareness grew, so did his desire to help others. Before he knew it, he was organizing workshops on his college campus. He started helping young people find answers. And he started finding immense joy while doing so. He constantly travelled and organized workshops in even more locations. While they were time-consuming, they were insufficient. He realized that many people learn from games. He decided to be a creator and ended up creating a product named Ikiguide, which is a series of insightful questions to help you discover who you are, where you want to go and how to get there. This helped him scale the impact he could deliver.

Nihal moved to Canada next, so that he could learn more in this area. It was not easy at first, with no circle and a completely different culture. Nihal specifically wanted to learn to solve complex problems at a policy level as he felt that many efforts to address societal issues focused on treating symptoms rather than addressing root causes. In short, he wanted to be a catalyst for systemic change.

A few years ago, when Nihal was finding it hard to even go to the classes on his campus, he could not have imagined himself moving to another country to study. But such was the power of mentorship that it gave him the tools to discover himself and find his purpose in life. All it took was sharing his need with a friend.

In 2025, mentors in India serve as vital emotional anchors for entrepreneurs, providing not just strategic guidance but also the much-needed emotional support. They help entrepreneurs navigate the unique cultural, societal and financial pressures that come with building a business in India's fast-paced and evolving startup ecosystem. From offering perspective during challenging times to helping them manage stress, mentors ensure that entrepreneurs have the emotional fortitude to succeed.

A Founder Should Always Be in Sales Mode—Really?

Shishir Modi was one of the founders of a technology startup, Niki.ai. His uncle was a successful businessman and his initial guide. When Shishir went to him to bounce off the idea of starting his own business, it garnered immediate support, leading to a tempting investment offer secured from him. However, Shishir, prioritizing professional boundaries, declined. He didn't take any further guidance from his uncle, as he wasn't sure how to face him after rejecting the investment offer.

For many years, Shishir did not try to get mentorship from anyone. He would approach mentors solely because it would add gravitas to the company profile. His interaction with mentors was primarily transactional. He would be in 'sales mode' with mentors as well. He feared that if he did not paint a good picture, the mentors would disappear. He wouldn't go to them with a problem and wouldn't be vulnerable to them. He always saw them as external stakeholders. When someone resigned and/or he couldn't hire competent people, it felt like a personal failure. Despite having sleepless nights, he didn't discuss any of his difficulties with his mentor.

This approach, while understandable, hindered Shishir's growth. He missed out on the invaluable insights and support that a mentor can provide. It wasn't until he connected with a personal mentor that he began to see the value of vulnerability. His mentor helped him understand that setbacks, such as resignations, were not personal reflections but rather a natural part of business.

Over the years, Shishir says that he discovered a crucial balance: while 80 per cent of a founder's time is spent selling the vision and the product, the remaining 20 per cent is equally important for self-reflection and seeking guidance. He now believes that a founder must be selling 80 per cent of the time and be vulnerable 20 per cent of the time.

But What Happens When You Don't Have a Mentor?

If someone shared with you that your current trajectory will lead you to miss out on your goals, would you continue doing what you are doing today?

Vijayananda Prabhu was the co-founder of a hospitality startup called Linger. He started his career with Infosys in the mid-1990s and spent over two decades there. One day, he accidentally took up entrepreneurship along with his friend. Linger is in the business of selling memories. With its motto of 'do nothing', it provides a unique leisure travel experience through many offbeat properties. Vijay wanted to provide an experience that he always craved for.

An experience where he wouldn't have to worry about check-ins and payments, about what to eat and what to do. Leisure in its truest form, where the vacation starts as soon as you leave your home. It was a 'soul business' for him.

Born into a service-class family, Vijay comes across as someone who is very approachable and ready to help others. He was always a problem-solver. Around 2010, one of his friends was building a retirement home for himself. On an online forum, his friend posted about taking his bathroom tiles to Chettimani in his Honda City. Vijay jumped in and added that he could use his jeep instead. They drove together, busted and changed a tire on the way and ended up sleeping in an unfinished house, all the while chatting about a potential business opportunity of converting the retirement house into an offbeat leisure stay. A month later, Vijay quit his job.

Over the next couple of years, Vijay got totally consumed by the business. He was the motherboard software taking care of all the execution. For instance, their manager did not show up once at their Kerala property. So, Vijay drove his bike all the way from Bengaluru to Kerala to be present at the venue to receive a guest in the evening.

The founders decided on the experience they absolutely 'did not want' to provide. They did not want to provide a reception and check-in. They did not want anyone to worry about individual costs, implying that it would be an all-inclusive package. They were one of the only homestays in those days with a 'no commerce' policy, which meant that you did not need to pay Linger for anything on the property. You could pay 50 per cent in advance and the rest later. This is before the UPI era, where one would need to add an NEFT beneficiary and wait for upto twenty-four hours to transfer money. Vijay would simply ask them to finish the vacation and pay later. This allowed them to change the focus of the staff to only hospitality. Their hospitality was such that they only had two issues of non-payment out of 10,300 bookings. Things were looking positive.

In the first three years, Linger managed to secure three properties without any capital investment. It was running on profits. The business model was such that they were utilizing dormant properties—those that were only eating up maintenance money for the owners without giving any returns. The founders realized that the model was working and had a decent profit margin, hence decided to accelerate. They went from four to fourteen properties in a year. While scaling up quickly, they ended up:

a)   Compromising on the fundamental success story of utilizing dormant assets.

b) Trying to experiment with investing upfront into the properties.

The scale-up led to doubling of the top line while reducing the bottom line and wiped out all the money in the bank.

Looking at other counterparts like OYO, they went to many venture capitalists (VCs) to raise capital. The feedback they received was that theirs was not a scalable business. A lifestyle business is not a VC play.

Meanwhile, they did not factor in the toll that the business was taking on their personal finances. They were not even drawing a sustenance salary for themselves. After spending six years in the business, Vijay was really hurting for cash flow. In 2015, he found out that his younger son was autistic. This is when Vijay decided to jump off the ship to find a job for himself.

Looking back, Vijay feels that one of the top three mistakes they made was not to get any mentor in this journey. He thinks a mentor would have warned them what to watch out for:

a) A mentor or business advisor could have helped them in structuring the business model correctly.

b) A mentor could have helped them set boundaries around the costly experiments, which would have ensured the cash flow in the company remains healthy.

c) A mentor or an executive coach helps as a referee around co-founder conflicts.

d) A mentor helps in designing a support system around founders, especially for emotional needs.

e) A mentor could have helped in nudging Vijay to draw financial returns out of the business. By not doing that, Vijay was harbouring the illusion that the business was in the green, whereas it was not, given his market salary (he could have been earning decently in a corporate job). In 2013, Vijay had an option of choosing a B2B venture (which eventually got sold for a massive sum) that he could lead as a co-founder. He looks back in regret as he chose Linger instead, where his heart was. A mentor could have helped Vijay play out the scenarios logically and then make a decision, instead of getting carried away by emotions.

In our experience, we have seen that a mentor can ensure minimizing regrets in your career, which is the key to a sound sleep at night.

Exercise 1

Who are the people you can think of for mentorship? Find three of them on LinkedIn, reach out to them and have a conversation with each in the next ten days.

Exercise 2: How do you assess if someone can be the right mentor for you?

The 'Road Trip' Test

Steps:

1. Go on a drive with your potential mentors.
2. Answer the following:
   a) Were you comfortable discussing your biggest challenges with them?
   b) Did they listen and provide actionable insights?
   c) Did you enjoy their company, even outside of a professional setting?
3. If the answer to two or more is **'No'**, they might not be the right mentor.

Chapter 4

Crossing the Threshold

'The cave you fear to enter holds the treasure you seek.'
—Joseph Campbell

For an entrepreneur, there comes a time where they have set out on a journey, following their call to adventure and despite the resistance from within, with or without help from mentors, they decide to step forward into the unknown. This stage is called crossing the threshold.

The threshold itself is not a physical border, waiting for you to produce your passport or visa. It could be incorporation of your startup, securing the first round of funding or just deciding to go forth. Many entrepreneurs we spoke to allude to the fact that this is a mental barrier that you cross whether you are ready or not. A lot of startups end here because the entrepreneurs lack the quality needed to cross the threshold—courage.

Courage is not just being externally aggressive, but an innate quality where an individual decides willingly to confront fear, overcome obstacles and take risks in pursuit of their entrepreneurial goals. Courage is what has gotten humanity so far and separates success stories from stories that could have been.

Entrepreneurship, like we shared in the earlier chapters, is a pursuit of goals beyond availability of existing resources. And that takes courage! So much is uncertain in the early stages of the startup as well as throughout the journey. There are risks associated with a new business venture: What if it fails? What if it can't scale? What if it is outpaced by competitors? Combine these with the fear within, and it makes a deadly cocktail that ties up an individual in self-doubt and conflict.

The spark of entrepreneurship is often fuelled by a bold vision or the desire to solve a pressing problem. Yet, bringing that vision to life requires stepping beyond the comfortable confines of one's safety net. Entrepreneurs must bravely confront their fears of failure, financial instability and market acceptance. It is this courage that sets successful entrepreneurs apart from those who merely dream.

Moreover, the path of an entrepreneur is marked by numerous challenges and setbacks. Failed product launches, lost investors and ever-changing market forces can all test an entrepreneur's resolve. In these moments, resilience becomes crucial. The ability to learn from failures, adapt strategies and push through obstacles is what separates thriving entrepreneurs from those who give up.

Risk-taking is inherent in the entrepreneurial journey. When fear and self-doubt creep in, it takes immense courage for an entrepreneur to stay the course. They must cultivate unwavering confidence and be prepared to face rejection and cynicism from every angle—whether it be from investors, customers, competitors or even loved ones. The entrepreneurs we have spoken to have all mentioned facing critical turning points during their journey in various forms.

What Is the Craziest That Can Happen?

As Dharamveer (DV) was nearing the completion of his undergraduate course at IIT BHU, he was reflective on what he would do next. By now, he had started up his first venture, Bright Ants Gaming Studio. He was clear that his life goal was living life while making games. But with a ceramic engineering degree and most companies offering software development roles, he had low expectations. One of his friends found out that Zynga, the game design company, was coming to campus; he decided to attend their pre-placement talks.

The Zynga team held a quizzing session about their games and offered T-shirts and bags as giveaways.

Interestingly, all those goodies were won by a student who wasn't even eligible for the software development role—DV. He nailed all the questions and amazed the recruiters as well as the students. Zynga reached out to DV to join them not as a software developer, but as their youngest game designer. DV had only one expectation—to have the freedom to dress casually, which even included *chaddi* shorts, and he was happy he found a place that gave him this. Being in a game design role, his dream had come true; he could spend his time designing and playing games. However, he spent a short time at Zynga as destiny had other plans for him.

While he loved learning the ropes of a game designer, DV had taken the Common Admission Test (CAT) for fun without any coaching experience. He attempted all questions in a blaze of glory. He cleared it and got a call from IIM Calcutta. As expected, everyone around him thought his future was now 'secure' and DV had arrived in life. But he had other plans. He did not want to end up in the rat race eventually and aspired to create his own identity.

In his first week at IIM Calcutta, he opted out of placements. This was not a brash rebellion, rather a means to spend time doing what he liked, since he was being asked to devote four or five hours daily to placement preparation, CV reviews, lectures, etc. The college authorities were worried about why someone would not want a placement and counselled him about trying internships, at the very least. But DV was clear. Because of Bright Ants Gaming Studio, he had the experience of running a small startup as a student and was raring to go again. He had knowledge about the startup ecosystem, funding and also had an idea. Before that, though, free of expectations of a job, he set out to do what he had consistently been saying—'I just want to play games all day.'

He turned his attention to playing online poker. Poker has always been controversial as it is addictive and in line with gambling. DV wanted to prove that there was more to it. His innate ability to go forth and try when anyone says it is impossible kicked in. He started investing a small amount of $10 every day to test his hypothesis. When others were hesitating or waiting for instructions on how to clear internship offers, he stepped forward with initiative. Being the first to act in uncertain circumstances demonstrates leadership and bravery.

While his batchmates were preparing for an internship, he reached out to Aditya Agarwal, India's best poker player at that time. Aditya agreed to mentor DV if he started blogging about his poker playing experience. DV continued to play a hand every day and tried to prove it's not just blind luck. Two months later, he hit the proverbial jackpot and won $10,000. There was a method to the madness after all and DV proved it to himself. He was on top of the world and Dharamveer Singh Chouhan never called back home again for money.

Many people in DV's place would have spent that money on an overseas vacation but he decided to use it as a seed to cross the threshold of his startup. Unlike last time with Bright Ants Gaming Studio, when he went solo, this time he decided he is going to get his wolf pack with him.

From here on, DV thought, '*Sabse crazy kya ho sakta hai* [What is the craziest that I can do]?' You may have noticed IIMs helping their students get a job of Rs 1 crore per annum. DV decided he would do better—by creating many such jobs. A lot of entrepreneurship masterclasses encourage you to find the right product fit, look at the techno-economic landscape of a nation, etc. to decide where to start up, to leave aside your own aspirations to invest in an industry and market where a product or service would work. DV decided to start up in an industry that is an extension of him—travel. Founder gurus will also advise you, without any malice, that you should pick the right fit of roles to be your co-founders. DV believed you earn good friends in life and called up the two friends he was closest to from IIT, and a few friends from IIM. If he were to start up, it would be his dream company in the enviable travel industry with people he wanted to work with and most importantly, he would create a company that would let him do what he wanted in a job—in chaddi shorts!

People assume startup founders today decide on an idea and BOOM—overnight success! Looking at DV's trajectory, one can easily assume that could be the case. But when we spoke to DV, he mentioned how after his trip to Europe in his undergraduate years, he asked a basic question, 'Why can't backpacking hostels work in India?' He took two years to conduct thorough research on the subject. He showed us detailed reports that he studied on the travel industry, traveller behaviour, etc. and came to the conclusion, 'Why not?' The vision emerged from the mist—to create India's largest backpacker hostel chain.

With that thought, he decided to step forth from the shadows and become a full-fledged entrepreneur. He opened the first Zostel in his hometown, Jodhpur, aka the Blue City. As a B-school student, he decided to pursue a strategy that was not just ingenious but unheard of before. Startup founders normally reach out to VC funds or angel investors, but DV and team went after business plan competitions. They applied to competitions of the premier B-schools; given their comprehensive research combined with a strong team, they won every single one of them— it was a clean sweep! IIT Bombay, IIT Kharagpur, India Economic Forum, Wharton and Stanford were just a few of them. They raised a million dollars in a few months! With this, they opened Zostels across three cities and leaped across the threshold into that world of imagination and realization.

With a Little Help from My Friends . . .

Our seeker Mayur Sontakke took a trip to Vietnam, seeking connection and evolution. He came across many digital nomads, individuals who use technology to work remotely and have the freedom to travel and live in different locations. This 'tribe' valued freedom, flexibility and mobility. This was also the time Mayur met his future wife, Joy. As they explored Vietnam, they also came across communities of more digital nomads, who were able to work remotely but also had a good work-life balance, a community to evolve with while maintaining a low cost of living.

Before Covid-19, remote jobs existed but were less common and often limited to tech roles, design and some freelance work. Most companies preferred on-site work, seeing it as essential for collaboration and productivity, while remote work was viewed as a perk rather than a norm. Startups and freelancers had more flexibility to work remotely due to budget constraints and independence, but traditional businesses often feared productivity would suffer outside the office. The pandemic proved that remote work could be effective, with digital tools enabling communication and teamwork, which ultimately shifted remote work from a niche option to a mainstream model.

Pre-Covid, digital nomads had already carved out a lifestyle that combined remote work with travel, often leveraging freelance or tech-based roles that allowed for flexible hours and location independence. They adapted by working from co-working spaces, cafes and affordable short-term rentals in digital nomad hubs like Bali, Chiang Mai and Lisbon, where Internet connectivity and support networks for remote workers were established. These early adopters helped pioneer and normalize the tools and practices—like video calls and project management platforms—that later became mainstream when remote work surged during the pandemic.

As Mayur and Joy spoke to people, they realized working from home is isolating and distracting while going to work means fighting through traffic and higher costs. If there was a combination of the social life of office with the convenience of home, that would be the perfect combination. They threw this thought out into the universe. Would it be possible to do this? What would be a low-cost location with Internet access and nature? India and the potential it had in hosting digital nomads was the idea that was born.

However, while they had the idea, it was a monumental challenge to pull together the finances. Every penny counted as Mayur and his team worked tirelessly to make their dream a reality. After much deliberation, they settled on opening their co-working/co-living space in Goa, a place known for its vibrant atmosphere and diverse community. But Mayur knew he needed to save up before taking the leap.

In 2019, fate seemed to smile upon them when they stumbled upon a stunning property in Assagao, Goa. It was perfect for their vision, and they were determined to make it happen. Mayur started borrowing money from friends, knowing that this was an important threshold to cross—turning their dream into a tangible business.

However, just as Mayur's dreams were about to come true and his business was taking off, the world came to a screeching halt. It was June of 2020 when the pandemic hit. As people fled to their hometowns, Mayur watched helplessly as his once busy community became a ghost town. His plans for expansion and growth were put on hold indefinitely. He was worried.

Three months passed and then, something unexpected happened. Digital nomads from all over India started reaching out, seeking refuge at Mayur's co-working/ co-living space. The timing couldn't have been more perfect, but Mayur didn't have the funds to expand and accommodate these new guests.

Despite putting all his finances together, Mayur saw the potential for growth and success but lacked the means to fund it. The pandemic had hit startups hard and securing funding seemed nearly impossible. But where others may have given up, Mayur remained determined to find a way forward for his community and dream.

As if by some heavenly intervention, something magical happened in that moment. The iconic tune, '*I get by with a little help from my friends*' by the Beatles, began to play, reverberating through every fibre of Mayur's being. It was as if the universe itself was lending a hand. The community of digital nomads, united by their love for NomadGao, came together with a common purpose: to support and uplift Mayur. With determination in their hearts and technology at their fingertips, they organized online gigs, utilized social media platforms to spread the word about NomadGao, and even crowdfunded to ensure its success. It was a testament to the power of camaraderie and the boundless possibilities of a connected world. The community helped them go from a small place of five rooms to a network of four locations in three Goan villages with 34 rooms.

Mayur believes that one person who understands the value and vision of a venture is better than ten who don't. He has finally found his Fellowship, a close-knit group bound by shared values, mutual support and a common journey. With the amplified power of community, Mayur was able to finally bring his dream to reality. When you want to cross the threshold in an entrepreneurial journey, you are not alone. Seek out your allies and move ahead resolutely in building your venture.

Exercise

Identifying Your Entrepreneurial Allies

Objective: To help you identify potential allies in your entrepreneurial journey who can provide support, resources and guidance.

Step 1: Self-Reflection
- Take a moment to reflect on your business idea or venture. Write down what specific skills, knowledge or resources you currently possess and what you might need from others to succeed.

Step 2: Create a Mind Map
- Draw a mind map with 'Allies in Entrepreneurship' at the centre. Branch out into different categories such as:
  - Family and Friends
  - Professional Contacts
  - Industry Peers

- Mentors and Advisors
- Community and Networking Groups

Step 3: Brainstorm Potential Allies

- For each category, list specific individuals or groups who could be potential allies. Consider:

  - Family and Friends: Who is supportive of your entrepreneurial aspirations?

  - Professional Contacts: Who from your network could offer insights or connections?

  - Industry Peers: Are there colleagues or fellow entrepreneurs you admire?

  - Mentors and Advisors: Who do you know that has experience in your field?

  - Community Groups: Are there local organizations or online communities that align with your business?

Step 4: Evaluate Relationships

- For each person or group listed, assess:

  - Interest in Your Idea: Do they show enthusiasm for your venture?

  - Relevant Skills or Experience: Can they offer valuable insights or connections?

- Willingness to Support: Are they likely to be approachable and open to collaboration?

Step 5: Action Plan

– Choose two or three individuals from your list to reach out to. Craft a brief message expressing your interest in discussing your venture and how you think their support could be mutually beneficial. Schedule a coffee chat or virtual meeting to explore potential collaboration.

The Inspired Leave Home

Mayank Jain had completed engineering from NSUT Dwarka, a renowned engineering college. He had a stable job and came home to parents who were happy that he was in the safe cocoon of family But Mayank was restless. He wanted to leave this sheltered life and transform himself further by applying himself at the grassroots level in the development sector.

Your call to adventure is always waiting for you to act on it. You might refuse once or twice but once you have decided that it is time to cross the threshold, your destiny begins. In Mayank's case, his destiny was to catch a train to Gaya, where his co-founder was based. Mayank wanted to make a social impact and this was not possible with a corporate job, where he could only do something on weekends.

It takes immense courage for someone to step off the well-trodden path, especially when it means leaving behind the expectations of family and community. For Mayank, being from a middle-class background made this decision even more difficult. The security of a stable, regular salary—a cornerstone of middle-class life—offered a sense of comfort that was hard to let go. The weight of unfulfilled familial hopes loomed large, and the guilt of stepping away from a predictable life was always present. But deep within, Mayank knew that true growth required this leap into the unknown.

He realized that his personal evolution could only take place beyond the confines of societal expectations, in a space where he could carve out his own path. With conviction, he chose to embrace the uncertainty, believing that in this very act of courage, he would discover his fullest potential. Confident, Mayank says two types of people do entrepreneurship—the first type is people who do not have an option (*majboor*) and the second type is the ones who are inspired (*prerit*). Everyone else chooses a stable job!

While there was significant resistance from his family, urging him to reconsider, Mayank was resolute in his decision. Like the Buddha, who left behind a life of comfort and familial duty to seek deeper truths, Mayank chose to venture into the unknown. He understood that stepping away from the familiar was not just an act of defiance, but a necessary step towards his own awakening. In a symbolic and perhaps subconscious alignment with the Buddha's journey, Mayank decided to travel to Bodh Gaya—the very place where Siddhartha Gautama had attained enlightenment under the Bodhi tree. It was a place where history, spirituality and personal transformation converged, and for Mayank, it felt like the right destination to confront his own inner darkness and seek clarity. Just as the Buddha had sought liberation from the constraints of worldly existence, Mayank hoped that in Bodh Gaya, he too would find the insight and peace to guide his own path forward. What awaited him there was sleeping on the floor, dealing with storms and floods and starting a journey that would transform him and the agriculture in that region for times to come. Mayank had crossed his threshold!

Exercise

Are you struggling to discover your true entrepreneurial passion? Try this simple, yet powerful activity:

1. List Your Passions (5 mins):

   Take a few minutes to jot down all the things you love doing. These can be activities that make you lose track of time, topics you enjoy reading about or causes that ignite strong emotions within you. Don't hold back; let your thoughts flow freely.

2. Identify Your Skills (5 mins):

   Next, make a list of your top skills. These can be talents that come naturally to you, or abilities you have acquired through work experience, education or hobbies.

3. Find Market Gaps (5 mins):

   Look into industries or areas related to your passions and skills. Pay attention to problems people are facing, unmet needs or consumer frustrations. These could be potential opportunities for an entrepreneurial venture.

4. Connect the Dots (5 mins):

   Now, take a closer look at where your passions, skills and market needs intersect. Is there a particular problem that aligns with your skills and excites you? This could be a sign of your true entrepreneurial passion.

5. Test the Idea (Optional):

    If you have identified a potential passion, try testing it out first. Start small by creating a prototype, offering a service or seeking feedback from others. This will help you determine if this path feels right for you.

By completing this exercise, you may uncover your authentic entrepreneurial passion and gain clarity on what to pursue next.

Market Rules!

According to CB Insights, 42 per cent of startups fail because there is no market need. One of the top venture capitalists in the world, a16z talks about how the market matters most. A great market—with lots of real potential customers—pulls the product out of the startup. The market needs to be fulfilled, and the market will be fulfilled by the first viable product that comes along. The product doesn't need to be great; it just has to basically work. And the market doesn't care how good the team is, as long as the team can produce that viable product.

TOP 20 REASONS STARTUPS FAIL
Based on Analysis of 101 Startup Post-Mortems

Source: CBInsights

In short, customers are knocking down your door to get the product; the main goal is to actually answer the phone and respond to all the emails from people who want to buy. And when you have a great market, the team is remarkably easy to upgrade on the fly. This is the story of search keyword advertising, Internet auctions and TCP/IP routers.

Conversely, in a terrible market, you can have the best product in the world and an absolutely killer team, and it doesn't matter—you're going to fail. You'll break your pick for years, trying to find customers who don't exist for your marvellous product; your wonderful team will eventually get demoralized and quit and your startup will die. This is the story of videoconferencing, workflow software and micropayments.

The #1 company-killer is a lack of market.

- When a great team meets a lousy market, the market wins.
- When a lousy team meets a great market, the market wins.
- When a great team meets a great market, something special happens.

You can obviously screw up a great market—and that has been done, and not infrequently—but assuming the team is baseline competent and the product is fundamentally acceptable, a great market will tend to equal success, and a poor market will tend to equal failure. **Market matters most.** And neither a stellar team nor a fantastic product will redeem a bad market.

Biswapati Sarkar, co-founder of Posham Pa Pictures, a renowned writer and actor, understood the importance of the market very early. While he was studying at IIT Kharagpur around a decade ago, he observed that cameras are becoming cheaper in India. He also observed that around 2012–13 onwards, YouTube India actively started promoting creators. He could see that the OTT market was poised to grow in India in the coming years. He decided to ride on this trend and joined TVF (The Viral Fever) to create videos over the Internet. His first video for TVF as a writer was 'Rowdies – Sab Q-tiyapa hai!', which became hugely successful. Over the years, he wrote shows like S1 and S2 of *Permanent Roommates*, S1 of *TVF Pitchers* and S1 of *Kaala Paani*, gaining immense popularity over the Internet.

While Biswapati was riding this trend, many people in the industry did not see it. He says in disbelief that even until 2018, he used to attend panel discussions where panelists would discuss if the Internet and web series were the future for the entertainment industry. To him, it was already the present! He was already on the other side of the threshold.

Bombay Monsoons

In the first two years of launching his startup, Devashish was cash-crunched. He used to travel to office daily taking a one-hour ride on his eight-year-old motorcycle. The monsoons of Mumbai are renowned for their intensity. It rains almost every day and creates havoc in the city. Devashish would put on two raincoats to safeguard himself while going to the office. Given the rain, he couldn't wear goggles to cover his eyes, so the view would not be clear. The roads were dangerous to drive on and one could easily get into an accident or slip into a drain. By the time he reached the office, he would be 70–80 per cent drenched from the rain. His shirt and jeans would be dripping with water. Air would flow through him as he stood in the parking lot, making him cold. In that moment, he felt—*what am I doing?*

It was widely covered in the media that he had received a Rs 1 crore salary from campus. He dropped that and chose to become an entrepreneur. He couldn't afford a car or stay near his office. After one year, he started drawing a Rs 10,000 salary. By the third year, he could afford to rent a small place near the office. Till then, he would be saving every penny and coming to the office drenched—while his batchmates from IIM had started living really comfortable lives. On some days, it would become really depressing for him. This made him rethink—am I really doing the right thing?

Looking back, Devashish reflects that Mumbai monsoons simply presented him with a miserable circumstance in the moment, but the mind would connect the misery to the decisions that he had taken—*if I would not have started a business, I would be sitting in Wall Street, living in a comfortable house, driving a car, always be in an AC environment and never have any drop of rain drench me*. But in due time, he realized that it was the environment that was making him doubtful. So, he decided to take charge and change his environment. Of course, he could not protest to stop the Mumbai monsoons. But he started keeping an extra pair of clothes in the office. He would change into clean dry clothes as soon as he reached. He installed a good AC in the office. With clean clothes and a good AC, he would feel the same way he may have felt sitting in Wall Street. His co-founder got a second-hand car and now they would go to meetings without getting drenched. By changing this environment as fast as possible, he could move on from his doubts and focus on the business. This was a small but important step in crossing the threshold for Devashish.

Crossing the Threshold with Trust

Sometimes, you might have incredible talent but to cross the threshold, you need the right allies. Alicia Souza and her co-founder's partnership was the perfect blend of creativity and pragmatism, two contrasting yet complementary forces that came together to build a successful business. Their journey as co-founders began in the most serendipitous way, and their story is a testament to the power of shared vision, complementary skills, trust and open communication.

Alicia, a quirky and talented illustrator, had always dreamed of creating something more than just an art portfolio. Her dream was to bring joy into everyday moments through her unique, playful designs. Whether it was whimsical doodles on notebooks, cheerful illustrations on planners or light-hearted quotes that resonated with people, she wanted her art to connect with the world on a larger scale.

Her co-founder, on the other hand, came from a business background, with years of experience in manufacturing. He had an eye for spotting trends and knew how to turn ideas into profitable ventures. His dream had always been to build a company that combined creative freedom with sound business strategy. He saw immense potential in the emerging space of lifestyle brands and products built around art and personality.

In India, many brands in the creative field are built around the names of visionary founders, whose personal artistry and unique aesthetic define the brand's identity. From fashion to architecture, art, and decor, these names carry significant influence as they embody the creator's style, legacy and cultural impact. Icons like Sabyasachi Mukherjee, Tarun Tahiliani and Ritu Kumar have transformed their names into brands that symbolize Indian luxury and craftsmanship in fashion. Meanwhile, architects and artists such as Bijoy Jain of Studio Mumbai and M.F. Husain have created brand identities rooted in their own art forms, with names that resonate globally. These brands often blend traditional Indian techniques with contemporary design, showcasing the founders' artistic roots and making their personal visions accessible to a broader audience.

When Alicia and her co-founder first crossed paths with an exchange of mails, they quickly realized how perfectly their visions aligned. Alicia had the artistic talent and a growing fan base, while her co-founder had the business acumen and experience to scale creative projects into profitable ventures. Over coffee, they shared ideas about how art could transcend traditional boundaries, finding its way into people's daily lives through products that were not just beautiful but also functional. They both envisioned creating a brand that celebrated everyday joy.

With this alignment, they knew they were onto something special. They decided to join forces and founded a company focused on selling products designed by Alicia—everything from stationery and calendars to lifestyle goods that embodied her cheerful art style. Their goal was simple yet powerful: to create a brand that people would associate with happiness and lightheartedness.

From the beginning, their partnership was defined by a strong balance of complementary skills. Alicia was the creative genius behind the brand, spending hours drawing, sketching and ideating the next big design that would resonate with their audience. She had a knack for capturing small moments of happiness and turning them into vibrant illustrations.

Her co-founder, Saurabh Sharma, on the other hand, was the strategist. He handled the business front—operations, marketing and logistics. He was always thinking about scalability, market positioning and how to translate Alicia's creativity into a profitable business model.

Saurabh understood the importance of nurturing Alicia's creative freedom while also ensuring that the business side remained structured and efficient.

Their complementary skills worked like a well-oiled machine. While Alicia would spend hours in her studio perfecting new designs, Saurabh would be in meetings with suppliers, negotiating deals or brainstorming the next big marketing campaign. Saurabh also brought a sense of discipline and focus to the creative chaos that often surrounded Alicia's world. He created systems and processes that allowed Alicia to focus on her art while the business side grew steadily.

Despite their different roles, one thing that set Alicia and Saurabh apart as co-founders was their commitment to open communication. From day one, they decided that transparency and honesty would be the foundation of their partnership.

Whenever they disagreed, they made it a point to listen to each other's perspectives. Alicia respected Saurabh's understanding of the market, and Saurabh valued Alicia's creative instinct. Their communication was never about proving the other one wrong or right but about finding the best way forward for the company and their shared vision. Alicia knew if she did not meet her deadlines, Saurabh would not be able to pay his team. And on the other hand, if there were issues with the supply chain or delivery, she would have to trust him.

This culture of open dialogue helped them navigate tough decisions. When they needed to invest in new product lines or expand their team, both were able to express their concerns openly. Alicia's fear of losing creative control was balanced by her co-founder's reassurance that every business decision would be in line with their brand's core values.

At the heart of their collaboration was an unshakable trust. Alicia trusted Saurabh to make the right business decisions, knowing that he always had the brand's best interests at heart. Saurabh, in turn, trusted Alicia's creative instincts and her ability to connect with their audience on a deeply personal level.

There were moments when the business faced challenges—production delays, budget constraints and the pressures of scaling quickly. Yet, they never doubted each other's dedication. When Alicia was unsure about a new design direction, Saurabh's steady confidence in her abilities kept her going. When Saurabh was overwhelmed by the operational demands, Alicia's unwavering belief in his leadership helped him push through.

This journey of co-founders is a story of perfect harmony between creativity and strategy. Their alignment of vision, complementary skills, open communication and deep trust formed the foundation of a successful partnership. Together, they built a brand that not only brought joy to people's lives but also stood as a testament to the power of collaboration.

Through ups and downs, disagreements and victories, they remained each other's greatest supporters. Their story was a reminder that in the world of business, the strongest partnerships are those where both parties bring their unique strengths to the table, align on their goals and, most importantly, trust each other as they cross the threshold.

As seen through various lenses, one can have a range of challenges and obstacles before they set forth on the journey of entrepreneurship. Initial inertia pulls you back but you step forward nevertheless. This marks the beginning of the most exciting phase of entrepreneurship. And as you cross this initial threshold, it's safe to say that *things just got real*. An entrepreneur must be agile and adaptable, ready to tackle any hurdle that comes their way with creativity and determination, no matter how big or small.

This journey is a marathon, not a sprint; therefore, persistence and courage are crucial in defining an entrepreneur. They must show up every day with bravery, because they have chosen to walk into the trials and tribulations of the entrepreneurial path. Taking the leap of faith is a defining moment for any entrepreneur as it represents a shift from just an idea to taking actionable steps towards building a business. This leap requires a blend of vision, resilience, courage and a deep understanding of the inherent risks involved. It also demands confronting the possibility of failure and the uncertainty that comes with venturing into uncharted territory.

At the core of this decision lies a compelling vision—an idea or solution that an entrepreneur believes can add value. This vision serves as their driving force to take risks. Entrepreneurs invest countless hours refining their ideas, researching the market and developing a strong value proposition. When they finally decide to act, it's because they have nurtured a strong belief in their concept and its potential to solve a real problem or fulfill a genuine need. This conviction becomes their anchor, providing clarity and focus to navigate the turbulent waters of entrepreneurship.

Courage plays an essential role in taking this leap of faith. The fear of failure can be overwhelming, coupled with concerns about financial instability, damage to reputation or disappointing loved ones. However, courageous entrepreneurs understand that the potential rewards of success far outweigh the risks of failure. They embrace failure as stepping stones towards growth and improvement. This mindset allows them to push past their fears and fully commit to their journey.

Ultimately, taking the leap of faith is a complex decision that intertwines vision, resilience, courage and support. It requires a deep belief in one's idea and the determination to face inevitable challenges. For many entrepreneurs, this leap is not just about starting a business, it's about pursuing a passion, making an impact and realizing their potential. In doing so, they inspire others to chase their own dreams, proving that the leap of faith can lead to extraordinary journeys and transformative outcomes.

Exercise

Note down an incident from last month when you felt fear. It could be something relatively small to start with. Close your eyes, take a deep breath and vividly imagine the fear or challenge. See the details, feel the emotions and acknowledge any anxiety or discomfort. Now, mentally visualize facing this fear with courage and confidence. Visualize a solution that was possible in that moment of fear. Imagine the fear resolving into a positive outcome and focus on how you would feel on overcoming the challenge. Start with small fears but consistently do this once a week for four weeks.

Chapter 5

Trials and Temptations

The journey of an entrepreneur is full of uncertainties and situations that test their resilience, creativity and integrity through the journey. From a psychological point of view, given that entrepreneurs operate in environments characterized by high levels of uncertainty, they are challenged more than individuals in other professions to have tolerance for ambiguity and the ability to make tough decisions in uncertain conditions.

Entrepreneurship is like a mirage where you think you know what is on the horizon but once you reach there, there are many dragons and monsters to slay. These come in the forms of challenges of managing people and finances, managing risk and scale and the pressures on mental health and biases. We will explore these through stories in this chapter.

Trials and Temptations of Being Human

What makes entrepreneurship thrilling and challenging is that one needs to be able to make critical decisions while demonstrating emotional intelligence. Building and maintaining relationships with team members, investors, customers and other stakeholders all decide the fate of a startup; entrepreneurs are tested on their people skills throughout the journey.

People are the backbone of any business, but finding and retaining the right talent can be a daunting task for entrepreneurs. They must compete with bigger and more established companies for skilled workers, and they have to deal with attrition, conflicts and performance issues. Entrepreneurs also need to balance their own roles as leaders, managers, mentors and visionaries, while maintaining healthy relationships with their co-founders, partners, investors and customers.

When You Are a Startup Founder, It Is Possible You Might Weep a Little!

Nitin Babel was the co-founder of Niki.ai. It was the spring season in Bengaluru. He had an early start that day. There was a morning meeting at the office with a potential investor from 7–8 a.m. The meeting went well, which helped raise his spirits, and he was looking forward to the day, which then suddenly turned on its head. He received news that one of his team members had passed away!

He was shocked! She was twenty-three and part of his marketing team. A bright professional, who started as an intern, she had just gotten into a full-time role. She came from a small town in Rajasthan. They had just met the previous day.

He simply rushed to the hospital with his team, where they met a couple of her flatmates—very young people who looked completely stunned. The doctors said it was a heart attack, and we had lost her even before she reached the hospital.

Everybody seemed completely lost around him. He had to take hold of the situation. They informed her father. There was no direct flight from the small town to Bengaluru and he would only be able to reach by evening. Meanwhile, they had to work with the police and the hospital to get all the papers in place, so that the body could be taken to Rajasthan. Nitin and his team decided to take it up.

When her father arrived, his eyes were red, and he was crying his heart out. He was crying on Nitin's shoulder in the hospital compound. Nitin was a twenty-seven-year-old entrepreneur—no business course teaches you what to do in these situations.

Once they came back to the office, nobody in the team had gone home. Everyone was waiting for them. Nitin informed them of what happened. He was in tears at that all-hands meeting. Never had he thought that he would be communicating about the demise of a team member.

An entrepreneur's journey teaches you a lot. Certain areas we may know about, but there are many that are blind spots to us when we take the journey. This got reinforced to Nitin that day—a startup is not just about working with people, but about genuinely knowing each other and being there for one another. It matters to have an emotional bond with your team and create a culture of care within the company. After all, you are a human first and an entrepreneur later.

Exercise

Entrepreneurship is often romanticized as an exciting journey filled with innovation, success and fulfillment, like so much of this book does. However, beneath the surface, entrepreneurs frequently encounter significant mental health challenges that can impact their well-being and ability to navigate the complexities of running a business. So many entrepreneurs have so much to juggle, the multiple priorities in tasks they have set out to achieve. As an entrepreneur, one may seem calm and collected on the outside, but behind closed doors, there is often a look of exhaustion and stress etched onto their face. They may appear to have it all together, but their eyes show the weight of their constant worries and thoughts.

A simple exercise that can make you self-aware, entrepreneur or not, is mindful breathing:

1. Set aside a few minutes each day to focus solely on your breath.
2. Set a timer of 3 minutes. Sit comfortably with your back straight, close your eyes and take slow, deep breaths.
3. Notice the sensation of the breath entering and leaving your body. Whenever your mind starts to wander, gently bring your focus back to your breath.
4. When the timer rings, gently open your eyes. You are present.

A practice like this helps you build attention to your thoughts and refresh yourself even on a busy day.

Deep, intentional breathing activates the parasympathetic nervous system, which is responsible for the body's rest and relaxation response. This can counteract the effects of stress and promote a sense of calm and well-being. Concentrating on the breath hones the skill of sustained attention and strengthens mindfulness. Mindfulness involves observing experiences without judgement. Focusing on the breath provides a neutral object of observation. When distractions arise or the mind wanders, practitioners practice acknowledging these experiences without criticism or attachment, fostering a non-judgemental attitude. As the mind inevitably wanders, entrepreneurs learn to gently redirect their focus back to the breath, strengthening their ability to concentrate. And once you practise controlling the mind, you have a better chance of dealing with the various challenges that come your way.

You Don't Need an IITian to Solve Every Problem!

Mayank's organization SumArth wanted to improve the income of thousands of farmers who grew mushrooms in Bihar. SumArth would provide them with training, seeds and market linkages. But he faced a big challenge: how to collect the surplus mushrooms from the farmers and distribute them to the NGO's centres, where they could be processed and sold. He tried hiring an IITian, who was a supply chain expert (given that IITians are supposed to know all the answers), but he was unable to continue after a few months. It was a misfit for both parties. Mayank was about to give up when he met Abhishek, a bus conductor.

Abhishek had been working as a bus conductor for over a decade. He knew every bus route and timing in Bihar like the back of his hand. He also had a good rapport with the drivers and passengers. He offered to help Mayank with his problem. He devised a simple and ingenious solution: he asked the farmers to drop their leftover mushrooms in a designated bag at a specific time in a specific bus, which he would mark with a sticker. He then coordinated with the drivers and other conductors to ensure that the bags reached the centres safely and on time. He charged a nominal fee for his service, which was much lower than hiring a truck or a courier.

Mayank was amazed by Abhishek's idea and execution. He thanked him profusely and hired him as the supply chain coordinator. Thanks to Abhishek, the centre was able to collect and distribute more mushrooms than ever before, increasing every farmer's income. Mayank learned an important lesson as an entrepreneur: keep looking for the right fit for your team, you might find your answer in unexpected places.

Exercise: As a startup founder, you know that having the right team in place is crucial for success and can make or break startups. To build the best team possible, follow these steps:

1. Identify Your Startup's Needs: Before you start recruiting, make a list of the roles and skills your startup needs to thrive. Consider what areas you may need help in and what specific expertise is required.

2. Create a Compelling Vision: A strong vision is essential for attracting like-minded individuals who are passionate about your startup's mission. Clearly communicate your purpose, goals and values to attract team members who share your vision.

3. Network and Connect: Attend industry events, join startup communities and network with professionals who have the skills and experience you're looking for. Building relationships with

potential team members before you need to hire can make the process smoother.

4. Embrace Diversity: Seeking out diversity in backgrounds, perspectives and experiences can bring valuable insights and creativity to your startup. Look for candidates from different backgrounds, who can offer fresh perspectives and contribute to innovation. A diverse team helps you look at a problem from different angles and share fresh solutions.

5. Evaluate Soft Skills: While technical expertise is important, don't overlook the importance of soft skills such as communication, adaptability and problem-solving. Look for candidates who demonstrate a growth mindset, resilience and willingness to learn.

6. Assess Cultural Fit: Building a strong team culture is essential for long-term success. Evaluate candidates not only based on their skills and experience but also on their alignment with your startup's values, work ethic and communication style.

In the talent landscape today, one should look for actionable business skills rather than labels because increasingly, people are learning to use digital marketing to put themselves out there. By meticulously following each of these carefully crafted steps and approaching the hiring process with a strategic mindset, you have the power to build a team of talented individuals who are not only skilled in their respective fields but also share a strong dedication to your startup's mission. With this cohesive team by your side, success is more probable for your growing business venture.

Potential Hides in Unusual Corners

Harvard defines entrepreneurship as pursuit of a goal beyond resources controlled. Our ex-army major Devashish takes it a step forward and believes in situational entrepreneurship. For him, an entrepreneur starts a business, but along the journey, creates multiple entrepreneurs who lead in specific situations. One such example was Noble Mavely.

Noble had always dreamed of creating something that would make a difference in the world. He loved technology and innovation, but he felt stuck in his tech support job. He wanted to be a product manager, someone who could shape the vision and direction of a software product.

He wanted to work on something that would solve real problems for real people.

But no one gave him a chance. His current company only cared about his technical skills, not his creative potential. When he requested a change, they gave him the title of product manager, but his work was still the same as before: answering calls, fixing bugs and following orders. He felt frustrated and unfulfilled.

He decided to seek help from Devashish, who he knew was the founder of a startup. Noble thought he might have some insights or advice on how to become a product manager. Devashish was himself looking to pivot his startup from a recruitment services company to a platform for recruitment consultants.

Noble was surprised when Devashish invited him to join his team as a part-time volunteer. Devashish said he was looking for someone who could help him design and develop the platform. He said he didn't care about Noble's credentials or experience. He only cared about his passion and willingness to learn.

Noble was thrilled. He saw this as an opportunity to prove himself and learn from Devashish. He started coming in every morning for four hours before going to his regular job. He immersed himself in the world of product development. He researched the market, customers, competitors and trends. He sketched out ideas, wireframes, mockups and prototypes. He tested and validated his assumptions with feedback from users and stakeholders. He iterated and improved his designs based on data and insights.

He did all this on his own initiative, without guidance or supervision from anyone else. He was driven by his curiosity and enthusiasm. He was also motivated by the vision of creating a platform that would revolutionize the recruitment industry. He wanted to make it easier, faster and cheaper for employers to find and hire the best talent.

He worked like this for six months, without taking any salary. He didn't mind. He was learning more than he ever did in his previous job. He was also enjoying the challenge and the satisfaction of creating something from scratch.

By the time Devashish raised seed funding from investors, Noble had created the entire product roadmap for the platform. He had designed every feature and every page for the first two versions of the product. He had also documented everything in detail and presented it to Devashish, the rest of the team and the investors.

They were all impressed by Noble's work. They realized that he was not just a volunteer, but a valuable asset to the company. They decided to hire him as a full-time employee, and in parallel, started looking for a senior in product from startups/IITs/IIMs.

Noble continued to work hard and smart on the product development. He also started leading and mentoring other product managers and software developers who joined the company later. Devashish wasn't finding any suitable senior professional in product to come in and lead. Meanwhile, Noble became an expert and an authority on the product in the company. After two years, Devashish made Noble the head of product, as now he believed that no one could do this job better than Noble who knew the A–Z of the product.

Within four years, Devashish carried out a board resolution and made Noble a co-founder.

Noble's story is one of courage, persistence and passion. It shows how one can achieve one's goals even without subject matter expertise, but with access to opportunities and mentors. It also shows how founders can successfully create situational entrepreneurs in their business to overcome the various trials in the journey.

Whether you are a seasoned entrepreneur or aspiring to be one, there is one crucial skill that will determine your success: the ability to bring out the best in people. Unfortunately, many startups fail because they do not prioritize this aspect. With most startup founders being under the age of thirty, they often see themselves as powerful and inspiring leaders. However, what they truly need to embrace is the understanding that motivating and supporting others requires consistent effort and genuine belief in their team. A key strategy for achieving this is by focusing on the strengths and unique talents of each team member rather than dwelling on their weaknesses. By doing so, you can cultivate a thriving and motivated team that will drive your business towards success.

Exercise: Here is a small activity that you can share to encourage someone:

1. Set aside some quiet time and find a comfortable space where you won't be interrupted.
2. Begin by taking a few deep breaths to centre yourself and bring your focus to the present moment.
3. Reflect on a recent accomplishment or task where you felt particularly successful or proud. It could be something related to work or even a personal achievement.

4. Write down three specific strengths or qualities that you believe contributed to your success in that situation. For example, it could be your creativity, perseverance, attention to detail, teamwork, etc.

5. Take a moment to appreciate and acknowledge these strengths within yourself. Recognize the value they bring to your work and your overall well-being.

6. Now, think about how you can apply these strengths to future challenges or projects. Visualize yourself utilizing these qualities to overcome obstacles and achieve your goals.

7. Finally, write down one actionable step you can take today to leverage one of these strengths in your work or personal life.

8. Take another deep breath and congratulate yourself for taking the time to recognize and celebrate your strengths.

Remember, each person possesses unique strengths and abilities. By acknowledging and nurturing these qualities, you can continue to grow and thrive in your professional and personal endeavours. Keep believing in yourself and the contributions you bring to the table!

Fuelling the fire within each member of your team is crucial for cultivating a high-performing and harmonious work environment. When individuals feel genuinely encouraged and valued, their drive and dedication soar to new heights. They become unstoppable forces, fuelled by a burning passion to succeed. Encouragement not only elevates spirits and instills confidence, but it also fosters an unbreakable bond amongst teammates. By acknowledging and applauding successes, offering constructive criticism and providing unwavering support during tough times, you create an unbeatable culture of synergy and camaraderie. The power of encouragement cannot be underestimated—it builds unshakable trust and fortifies relationships between team members, resulting in flawless communication and seamless cooperation. Ultimately, by igniting the flames of motivation within your team, you propel their personal and professional growth, unleashing a positive chain reaction that benefits both the individual and the entire team.

A Leader Is Allowed to Have Doubts

Phani was feeling hopeless. He had started redBus, an online bus ticket booking service, with his friends a year ago, but the business was not picking up. He had left a lucrative job to pursue his dream of entrepreneurship, but now felt like he had made a huge mistake. His co-founders were also struggling to make ends meet, and he felt responsible for their situation. He wondered if it was time to give up and look for another job.

He decided to call a meeting with his co-founders and break the news to them. He expected them to be angry or disappointed, but to his surprise, they were supportive and optimistic. Phani shared with them that while he was hopeful initially, he now had doubts if this was going to be a successful venture. One of his co-founders, Sudhakar Pasupunuri, said, 'Phani, we knew this was not going to be easy. We signed up for this because we believed in your vision and passion. We are not quitters. We are fighters. Any business takes years to build, not a few months. We have to be patient and persistent. We are not going anywhere.'

Phani felt a surge of emotion as he heard these words. He realized that he was not alone in this journey. He had a team of loyal and dedicated friends who shared his dream and were willing to face any challenge with him. He felt a renewed sense of confidence and determination. He thanked his co-founders for their faith and encouragement and vowed to work harder and smarter to make redBus a success.

That meeting ended up being a turning point in the history of redBus. The company soon started to grow and attract more customers and investors. It became one of the most popular and trusted online bus booking platforms in India, serving millions of happy travellers across the country. Phani and his cofounders never looked back after that day. They proved that with the right set of co-founders, anything is possible.

Exercise

Selecting the perfect co-founders is a crucial and decisive element for any startup's success. It could even be likened to choosing a life partner—someone who will be by your side through thick and thin, supporting and complementing you in all aspects. When seeking a co-founder, it's important to find someone with skills and expertise that complement your own. For instance, if you excel in product development and technology, it would be beneficial to have a co-founder with a strong background in business or marketing. This diverse range of skills can greatly enhance problem-solving abilities and decision-making within the team.

However, it is also vital to ensure alignment in terms of vision. A co-founder should share your passion and be dedicated to achieving the same long-term goals as you are. Going back to the exercise on strengths, do the following:

1. List down your startup's three-year business goals.
2. Look at what strengths will be needed in co-founders to achieve those goals.
3. List down the strengths you think you possess.
4. The strengths and competencies that the founding team needs and what you think you lack is what you need to look for in a co-founder, whether it be conflict resolution, networking or creativity.

Remember, it's essential to carefully consider all factors and perform due diligence when selecting co-founders. With a strong founding team at your side, you can navigate challenges and work towards long-term success in entrepreneurship with confidence and determination.

Identity Crisis

Shishir had always been a driven individual, pouring every ounce of his energy into his startup, Niki.ai. From the moment the company was born, Shishir didn't just see himself as the founder; he became the company. The lines between Shishir Modi, the person, and Niki.ai, the startup, blurred until they were indistinguishable. This deep connection was both a source of strength and vulnerability.

In 2016, Niki.ai was still a small operation, with a close-knit team of just fifteen members. When a developer decided to resign—the first resignation the company had ever faced—Shishir felt it like a dagger to the heart. It wasn't just a professional loss; it was personal. For two sleepless nights, he agonized over what he perceived as a rejection of himself, not just his company. The incident left him questioning his abilities, wondering if he was somehow failing as a leader.

This feeling wasn't just confined to employee resignations. Every time an investor turned down an opportunity to fund Niki.ai, Shishir took it personally, as if the rejection wasn't just about the business but about him as a founder. Each 'no' from investors chipped away at his confidence, making him question his worth and the viability of his dream.

But the consequences of this merged identity didn't stop at emotional turmoil. The financial implications were just as significant. Shishir found it nearly impossible to separate his personal finances from the company's. He felt guilty about drawing a salary, as if taking money for himself was somehow robbing his company of resources. He sacrificed his time and energy, convinced that every rupee spent on himself was a rupee less for Niki.ai.

This financial entanglement also skews a founder's perception of success. For a founder who has not seen any wealth, even a small outcome of say Rs 20 crore for the business seems big. However, personal wealth creation, Shishir theorizes, could be a game-changer. A founder with a financial safety net could set bolder goals. Someone who has built a Rs 1 crore personal nest egg will aim for a Rs 500 crore valuation instead of settling.

But perhaps the most significant impact of this identity crisis was on Shishir's personal relationships. Like many founders, he took his family for granted, assuming they would always be there, just as focused on his dream as he was. Growing up, Shishir had been particularly close to his grandmother. She had been his confidante, his emotional anchor. However, once Niki.ai took off, Shishir became so consumed with the company that he stopped visiting home. The startup demanded his attention day and night, leaving little room for anything else.

Over a year passed without Shishir making the trip home. In the meantime, his grandmother's health deteriorated. She grew weaker, stopped speaking, and became a shadow of the vibrant woman Shishir had once known. When he finally did visit, the sight of her on drips was a stark reminder of the time he had lost. Despite her frailty, his grandmother mustered the strength to greet him with the same enthusiasm she had always shown. But just fifteen days later, she passed away.

Shishir's journey through this identity crisis wasn't just a personal struggle; it was a learning experience. He began to understand the importance of maintaining boundaries between himself and his startup. He realized that for Niki.ai to thrive, he didn't need to sacrifice his well-being, his finances or his relationships. In fact, doing so was counterproductive. A healthy founder, both mentally and financially, is better equipped to lead a company to success.

Shishir's story is a cautionary tale for entrepreneurs. It is a reminder that while passion and dedication are crucial for building a successful startup, they shouldn't come at the cost of personal identity, financial security or relationships. A founder is not just their company; they are an individual with their own needs, dreams and loved ones. By keeping these aspects of life in balance, founders can lead not just successful companies but fulfilling lives.

Hustle and Network—Even in Your Fifties!

Right after an entrepreneur has thought about the idea, the next step is to find the right people to put on the bus. This step could be a make or break for the startup. Every entrepreneur can't do everything alone and needs people to bring in their unique skills and energy that shape an early startup.

After Sangeeta decided to start her own venture in 2015 at the age of fifty, she was drifting towards her comfort zone—print media. Having worked for so many years in journalism, she was quite confident with the core aspect of the profession. While she could research and write stories, getting them out to the world is something this venture was about to teach her. It was at this point that her son advised her that this was the time of digital media; today's generation did not read print and any media house worth its salt had its own website and social media sites. Print readership was limited but access to digital content was growing rapidly. The shelf life of online stories was longer, too, and the reach was vast. Here came Sangeeta's Eureka moment—if she was to run a startup, it should be through digital means.

Sangeeta soon came to the realization that she could network, follow stories, take interviews, write stories and publish them. But she had no clue on how a website was created. This was when she reached out to an ex-colleague for help. The ex-colleague helped her connect with his network of UI designers and website developers. He recommended a good team and asked if she was willing to invest in the team. She put together some of her own money and jumped at the opportunity as she knew a good tech team is what would define success for her new venture.

The new team had an average age of twenties working with a founder in her fifties. We were amazed to see she had no qualms stating that she leveraged her gray hair and called her colleagues *beta* [son] so she could connect and make things happen. Sangeeta did not just delegate the tasks to the 'tech' team alone, but in her mid-fifties, learnt to upload stories on the website herself, past her team's working hours. This was a true example of the new talent coming to the rescue of old wisdom to create Aviation and Defence Universe (ADU). The young Turks worked with Sangeeta to brainstorm on various names, set up Search Engine Optimization (SEO) and buy domain names. Gradually, she built a team who is making a dent in the world of defence journalism even today.

Building the capability of the team was important, too. She had to train photojournalists on how to take pictures of a plane with the logo or what angle to take a picture of a General on stage. No work is limited for a founder as one has to coach and guide their team towards success, leading from the front.

She also reached out to her ex-students and former colleagues, who were journalists in Europe, the Middle East and Southeast Asia, who agreed to collaborate. This way, she not only gave a global workforce to the organization but also was able to save costs using the power of her networks. As an entrepreneur, you need to be able to lead and inspire others. Building a strong network of contacts is crucial. Networking skills involve the ability to establish and maintain relationships with people from various backgrounds, industries and levels of expertise. Effective networking allows you to access resources, gather insights and find potential partners, investors or customers. Even in this case, she encouraged her students who were not from the defence field to learn for themselves, make questionnaires and run interviews instead of spoon-feeding them. Teaching a journalist how to fish meant they would go out and fish for the best stories with the right bait.

Sangeeta leveraged the power of her professional networks to build her startup brick by brick. She thought of an ex-colleague of her father and husband, a Brigadier, to be the managing editor of the venture as she set out to be the founder–editor. He agreed and brought with him the legitimacy and experience of his life experiences. She also reached out to ambassadors, generals, admirals, air marshals, mid-level expert veterans and defence and aerospace industry professionals to be members of the board of advisors.

Entrepreneurs often need to collaborate with others to bring their ideas to life. Collaboration skills involve being open to different perspectives, respecting and valuing the contributions of others. Your network will not be used optimally until you ask for help. Experts are keen to share their guidance but only if you leave shyness at the door and go forth boldly with what you want to achieve. Effective collaboration enhances creativity, problem-solving and overall productivity. With the varied experiences that a diverse board brought in, she was able to write stories not just from a third-person perspective, but from the horse's mouth. This gave the content that ADU was putting out the depth it needed in a world of fast media.

With the right people on the bus, Sangeeta set out to conquer the universe of aviation and defence journalism.

Founder's Spirit Is a Blessing as Well as Bane

Limitless Institute, a beacon of personal and professional growth, is more than just an organization; it's an extension of its founder, Nihal Ahmed. His infectious enthusiasm, unwavering belief and deep-rooted purpose have become the driving force behind the institute's success.

Nihal's ability to inspire and motivate others is unparalleled. When he speaks, his eyes light up and his passion is palpable. His genuine commitment to helping people discover their potential resonates with clients, who are drawn to his unwavering belief in their abilities. This personal connection and authenticity are cornerstones of the success of Limitless. He is the biggest reason people buy.

However, the institute's rapid growth has presented a unique challenge. While Nihal's charisma and passion are undeniable, it can be difficult for others to replicate his energy and authenticity. For example, it is rare for Nihal to find sales representatives who can match the depth of connection and inspiration that he brings to the table.

This discrepancy between Nihal's personal brand and the broader Limitless experience at times hinders the company's ability to scale. While Nihal's charisma is a powerful asset, it's also a double-edged sword. It's a testament to his unique qualities, but it can also create a high bar for others to meet.

So, how can you create more leaders in your startup, who resonate with the same passion as you?

Exercise 1:

List three aspects of your area of work that have a high dependency on you.

Exercise 2

Team Workshop: Building Our Golden Circle Together

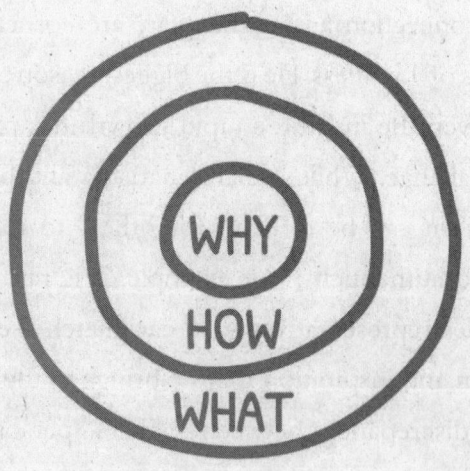

Objective: To collaboratively develop a shared 'Golden Circle' (Why, How, What) for our business, strengthening team alignment around purpose and vision. This exercise will help each team member connect with the company's mission and see their role in supporting it.

Workshop Outline

Duration: 1.5–2 hours

Materials Needed: Whiteboard or large paper, sticky notes, markers

1. Introduction to the Golden Circle (10 minutes)

Overview: Explain Simon Sinek's Golden Circle[3] framework:

- Why: The core purpose of the business—why it exists beyond making money?
- How: The unique approaches and values that make this purpose achievable.
- What: The products or services the business offers.

Goal for Workshop: Together, we will create our 'Golden Circle' to clarify our company's purpose, define our unique

---

3 Simon Sinek, *Start with Why: How Great Leaders Inspire Everyone to Take Action* (New York: Portfolio, 2009).

approach and establish what we offer. This will serve as a foundation for team alignment and inspiration.

2. Discovering Our 'Why' (30 minutes)

Step 1: Individual Reflection (5 minutes)

   — Prompt: 'In your own words, why does our company exist? Think beyond profit—what difference are we here to make?'

  Here are some examples:

   — Google: let's organize the world's information; Apple: let's reinvent the status quo

   — Instructions: Each person writes their thoughts on a sticky note (One or two sentences max).

Step 2: Group Sharing and Discussion (10 minutes)

   — Go around the room, with each team member briefly sharing their 'Why' statement. Place all sticky notes on the whiteboard under the 'Why' section.

Step 3: Identify Common Themes (10 minutes)

   — As a team, discuss common themes and keywords from the notes. Group similar ideas together, refining down to the most important points. For example:

- Are there recurring themes about user impact, innovation or social change?
- Facilitator's Role: Help the team identify and refine these themes into a concise, shared 'Why' statement that resonates with everyone.

Step 4: Finalize the 'Why' statement (5 minutes)

- As a group, agree on one powerful statement that captures the company's purpose. Write this on the whiteboard as your team's collective 'Why'.

3. Defining Our 'How' (30 minutes)

Step 1: Group Brainstorm (10 minutes)

Prompt: What values or unique approaches set us apart in fulfilling our 'Why'?

- Examples might include dedication to quality, innovative processes or a commitment to customer relationships.
- Each person writes two or three ideas on sticky notes, adding them to the 'How' section on the whiteboard.

Step 2: Discuss and Prioritize (10 minutes)

- Review all the 'How' notes as a team. Discuss the most impactful and unique approaches, grouping similar ideas.

– Select three to five core approaches that everyone
agrees represent the company's methods and values
in fulfilling its purpose.

Step 3: Craft the 'How' statement (10 minutes)

– Together, turn the selected approaches into a set
of statements or keywords that define 'How' the
company delivers on its purpose. Write these as a list
on the whiteboard.

4. Defining Our 'What' (20 minutes)

Step 1: Group Discussion (5 minutes)

– Prompt: What products or services do we provide to
our customers?

– Encourage the team to think about how these
offerings connect to the 'Why'.

Step 2: Simplify and Clarify (10 minutes)

– Together, craft a concise description of what the
company offers, ensuring it is easily understandable
and connects clearly with the 'Why' and 'How'.

– Write this 'What' statement on the whiteboard.

Step 3: Review and Align (5 minutes)

– Step back and look at the complete Golden Circle on the board (Why, How, What).

– Discuss any final adjustments to make sure the statements align and flow well together.

5. Closing and Reflection (15 minutes)

Reflection Questions for the Group:

– How does this Golden Circle resonate with you personally?

– How can we, as a team, use our 'Why, How and What' in day-to-day decisions to drive meaningful impact?

Next Steps

– Document the Golden Circle and share it with the team as a reference for decision-making, team alignment and external communication.

– Discuss ways to integrate this purpose into team meetings, goal-setting and onboarding materials for new team members.

By co-creating the Golden Circle, the team not only defines the company's purpose but also builds a collective sense of ownership and inspiration around the mission. This shared vision serves as a powerful motivator for fostering leadership and encouraging team members to embody the company's purpose in their work.

Bet on Culture Rather than Just Abilities

Building the right team and getting the right people on the bus is the not-so-secret ingredient for any startup. While there is a talent war heating up amongst big tech and product startups, the world is also heating up, quite literally. As countries around the world face challenges such as global warming, poverty and inequality in equitable access to healthcare and education, organizations such as Ankit Jain's are working on advising governments and philanthropies on governance transformation and development-centred programme delivery.

Ankit talks about the hiring challenges that a startup in the field of social impact faces. Given that the work being done by Ankit's startup is complex and multidisciplinary, the talent needed to perform in such an environment should also be able to solve complex problems, think creatively and drive impact on the ground. These competencies are required by top MNCs and big tech companies, too. What often happens is that Ankit and his team face challenges in attracting and retaining talent in the social impact sector as they are competing with very strong paymasters and benefits that they give.

What Ankit and team really need are motivated individuals who are passionate about the purpose of making a difference on the ground. Instead, among serious candidates, they also get a stream of Gen Z talent that does want to do development work, but only so that they can get diverse experiences on their CV and then apply to foreign universities. And are they to blame? For doing similar problem-solving, they will enjoy the perks of a comfortable life and socializing in cities rather than getting weathered in rural and bureaucratic India.

It is against this backdrop of the war for talent that I asked Ankit how he intends to carry on. He shares that when one can't attract talent with just compensation, career ladder or fancy offices, what you can give people is a vision—of a better world. The mission is to find people who care about that better world and are ready to roll up their sleeves.

Ankit and his team have a unique recruiting strategy. They not only conduct one-on-one interviews, but the team spends time with a candidate to figure out if the alignment with thoughts, values and actions are real and not just sales in an interview. When they find talent that aligns with their vision and culture, they join GDi and stick on, despite the ups and downs of the job. As Ankit puts it, '*Hum honge kaamyaab* [we will succeed]', and uniting to solve wicked problems only works when people are intrinsically motivated. They are few but the few will make an impact, just like Ankit.

Conduct Counts for Everything

For Biswapati, it was not easy to relate with entrepreneurship the way it was building up in India. He often felt out of place among the other entrepreneurs, who followed a philosophy of 'go big or go home'. He says that no creature or life form in nature says this, it's unnatural and artificial. He wondered why they were so obsessed with scaling up, raising funds and becoming unicorns, when he could see that they were under immense pressure and not happy. He felt that they were missing the point of entrepreneurship, which was to create something meaningful and enjoyable.

Biswapati has a different value system. He believes in Jeff Bezos's quote, 'If you can't feed your team with two pizzas, it's too large.' Biswapati values quality over quantity, depth over breadth and craft over speed. He prefers to work with a small team of talented and passionate people, who can collaborate and communicate effectively. He cares about the happiness and well-being of his team members, not just their productivity and performance.

He also believes that business should be ethical and humane, not ruthless and cut-throat. He hates when people just shrug off and say, 'This is how business is,' to justify their bad actions. He thinks that business should be a force for good, not evil.

Biswapati's value system was shaped by his love for writing and his admiration for Jiro Ono, the legendary sushi chef. Biswapati had watched the documentary *Jiro Dreams of Sushi* and was deeply moved by it. He saw himself in Jiro, who was obsessed with his craft and devoted his life to perfecting it. Biswapati felt the same way about writing. He loved every aspect of it, from brainstorming ideas to polishing sentences. He never took shortcuts or compromised on quality. He always strived to improve his skills and learn new things.

Jiro Dreams of Sushi changed Biswapati's life. It gave him a clear vision of what kind of creator he wanted to be. It also gave him confidence and validation for his style of work. Before watching the documentary, he sometimes doubted himself and wondered if he was crazy to go so deep into his craft. But after watching it, he realized that he was not alone or mad. He was just following his passion and purpose.

Biswapati's value system also influenced his company culture. At Posham Pa Pictures, nobody spoke harshly or hurled abuses at each other on set, a rarity in the film industry. The crew members were respectful and supportive of each other. They all worked hard but also had fun along the way. They enjoyed the journey as much as the destination.

Biswapati knew that his value system was different from the mainstream one. He knew that he might not fit in with the majority of entrepreneurs or filmmakers. But he did not care about that. He cared about being true to himself and his craft. He cared about creating stories that would touch people's hearts and minds. He cared about making a difference in the world through his work.

How to Find the Right Co-Founder

In his journey of building Limitless, Nihal has been a solo founder and, at one point, had a co-founder for four years. He shares that having a co-founder is similar to having a spouse. You spend half your day with that person, go through the ups and downs of the business together, have fights as well as celebrate the wins. Hence, it is no wonder that the success of a venture is highly correlated with a successful partnership between founders. In fact, one of the top reasons a startup fails in its early stages is co-founder conflict.

If that's the case, why did Nihal need a co-founder in the first place?

a. For Nihal, the first few years as solo founder were perfectly fine. But after a while, he started feeling that there are certain limits to his growth. He wanted someone to bounce ideas off, someone who would think differently and bring a new perspective. Someone who could become a growth partner.

b. Founders at times tend to drown in their own freedom. Nihal shares that as a founder, you have a lot of freedom, but sometimes you don't know what to do with that power. You can weed out people's voices and feedback and don't have anybody to hold you accountable. A co-founder helps keep this delusion in check.

c. He also wanted someone to share the load of adversities, fears and vulnerabilities.

So, what is Nihal's framework to identify the right co-founder?

a. Skill complementarity: Map out the things that you don't enjoy doing or that don't energize you. Nihal mentions that he is really good at being a creator, but not great at focus and scale. So, he would look for a co-founder with complementary skills.

b. Shared values and mindset: With respect to mindset, do our values align? As we know, for Nihal it is about more than just making money. He says that though it's not wrong to just be making money, in his case, a person who is willing to do whatever to make more money will not have alignment with his value system. A simple way to check for value system alignment: Is this a person you enjoy going on a road trip with? Is this a person you enjoy having a beer with?

c. Temperament compatibility: What's the breaking point of the other person? When do emotions take over rationality? Can you manage each other's breaking points?

Game: The Co-Founder Quest

Objective: To find the right co-founder for your entrepreneurial venture.

Gameplay:

1. **Character Creation:**
   - Choose your background (e.g. tech, business, creative.)
   - Determine your character's strengths, weaknesses, core values and breaking points (When do your emotions take over?)
   - Do the same for each potential co-founder.

2. **Exploring the World:**
   - Imagine navigating through different environments (e.g. mundane office hours, road trips, negotiation simulations, brainstorming new ideas.)
   - Interact together with various characters (e.g. potential employees, investors.)

3. **Completing Challenges:**
   - These challenges could involve team-building activities, problem-solving scenarios or ethical dilemmas.

4. **Making a Decision:**
   - Choose the co-founder who best aligns with your character's needs, values and temperament.

Trials and Temptations of Managing Finances:

Who You Take Funding From Matters!

Finances are another major source of stress for entrepreneurs. They have to constantly monitor their cash flow, expenses, revenues and profits, and make sure they have enough funds to sustain their operations and growth. They also have to deal with the uncertainty and volatility of the market, and the pressure from investors and creditors to meet their expectations and deadlines. Entrepreneurs must be careful not to overspend or underspend, and to avoid falling into debt or losing control of their equity.

Getting initial funding for your startup is a huge milestone for a young entrepreneur as it validates the product and market. It shows that you have a viable solution to a real problem and that there is a demand for it.

A cherry on the cake is when you bring in investment from your role model. It boosts your confidence and self-esteem as a young entrepreneur. It means that someone you admire and respect believes in your vision and potential.

Many entrepreneurs struggle with imposter syndrome and self-doubt when they start their journey. They feel like they are not good enough or qualified enough to run a business. Getting support from someone you have looked up to since childhood can help you overcome these feelings and embrace your identity as an entrepreneur. It can make you feel more authentic and legitimate in your role.

This is what Nitin experienced when he got funding from the legendary Ratan Tata. Tata is one of the most successful and respected business leaders in India and the world. He has built a global empire of diverse and innovative companies. He has also been a philanthropist and a mentor to many entrepreneurs. Getting funding from him was a dream come true for Nitin. It confirmed for Nitin that he had made the right choice by pursuing entrepreneurship.

Exercise to get connected with your heroes:

1. Make a list of ten heroes, with whom you would want to associate with your startup. Let's call it the 'heroes list'.
2. A warm introduction is one of the biggest levers to get a meeting with your heroes.
3. Identify and make a list of a hundred second and third connections that you have with your 'heroes list'. Let's call them 'well-wishers'. Observe that while it might have seemed daunting at first to get

    connected with your heroes, you might start seeing
pathways now.

4.   Set a target to meet one 'well-wisher' every week.
Enroll them into your story. Do this for at least ten
weeks. Observe that you will start converting 'well-
wishers' into 'believers'.

5.   Once you have five believers, make a bold request to
them to provide a warm introduction to your hero.

Creativity Does Not Pay the Electricity Bill

Once upon a time, in a small, vibrant neighborhood of
Bengaluru, lived Alicia Souza, a young and passionate
illustrator with a sketchbook full of dreams. She had
always loved drawing—ever since she could hold a pencil.
Her whimsical doodles filled the pages of every notebook
she owned, each character coming alive with quirky smiles,
bright eyes and an undeniable sense of joy.

But passion didn't pay the bills.

As a budding illustrator, Alicia faced a tough reality:
the creative field was not as nurturing as she had
imagined. Opportunities were scarce, corporate India
had not yet warmed up to illustrations (except for fun')
and the world wasn't knocking on her door asking for

cute characters or heartfelt doodles. In a country where art was often seen as a hobby rather than a career, her path was riddled with uncertainty.

Her struggles began right after she graduated from design school. Armed with talent but very little money, Alicia set out to find work in a market that seemed indifferent to her style. She took on small freelance gigs, designing logos, posters and book covers. The pay was meagre, just enough to cover her rent and art supplies. Many clients didn't fully value her work, offering exposure instead of compensation. But Alicia couldn't afford to stop; she kept going, sketching late into the night, her fingers smudged with ink and determination. She was running out of money but did not want to go back to her parents who were living in Abu Dhabi. Once her mother sent her some money and Alicia felt disappointed in herself as she didn't want her mother to know that she was struggling!

The creative ecosystem around her wasn't yet developed enough for someone like Alicia. People think that illustrators just wake up and start drawing whatever they feel like. At the time, illustrators were seen as secondary to graphic designers or animators, and the niche market for illustrated products, like the ones she dreamed of creating, didn't really exist in India. There were few platforms that supported independent artists.

Despite her setbacks, Alicia wasn't ready to give up. She started sharing her illustrations on Facebook. Being an introvert, it was not easy to put herself out there again and again. Slowly, people began to notice her unique style— characters full of warmth, with stories that felt personal and relatable. As she started delivering some work, word of mouth spread. Her quirky, endearing portrayal of everyday life struck a chord with people. It was through these small but significant online engagements that Alicia began to carve out a niche for herself.

As her audience grew, so did her confidence. She launched her own brand of merchandise, featuring her illustrations on everything from notebooks to mugs. Her products spoke to a generation that was yearning for something light, fun and joyful—a reflection of Alicia's own personality.

But her success didn't come without its share of hurdles. There were still moments of doubt. There were still long stretches of time when she was on a shoestring budget, and the uncertainty of the future loomed large. But Alicia had learned something through all her struggles: courage meant staying the course, even when it felt impossible. Creativity, for her, was not just a career but an act of resilience.

Years later, Alicia would look back on those early days—the late-night sketching sessions, the underpaid gigs, the empty bank accounts—and feel a deep sense of pride. What she once thought were her greatest challenges had turned into her greatest strengths. Her illustrations had found their place in people's hearts, and she had carved out a space for herself in an ecosystem that had slowly caught up with her.

Just Alicia's story is one of persistence, belief in the power of creativity and the courage to keep drawing when the world seemed unwilling to see her art. Through it all, she learned that success is not about how quickly you achieve your dream, but how fiercely you hold on to it, no matter how long it takes.

What Alicia adds is that it is better to have the right person on the job rather than the best person, because the right person aligns with the specific needs, culture and long-term goals of the role—organization or brief. While the 'best' person may have superior qualifications or experience on paper, they may not necessarily fit the unique demands of the position, or they may lack the adaptability required for the company's environment.

The right person understands the nuances of the job, collaborates effectively and contributes meaningfully to the team's dynamics. Ultimately, the right fit can drive lasting success and harmony, while the best may only excel in the short term. Alicia worked very hard to be that dependable person despite the talent she had—that is what sets her apart and is the key to her success.

Fail Fast

Mehul Jain is a multifaceted personality, who has explored various domains of knowledge and creativity. He is a prodigy with an All-India Rank of 5 in JEE. He started his career as a software engineer from IIT Bombay and then pursued an MBA from INSEAD. He founded Yogami. fit in 2021, a platform that connects yoga instructors and learners.

As an engineer, he learned how to design and build things with structure and boundaries, but he soon realized that marketing requires a different kind of thinking. He shared his trials with spending marketing dollars, which we commonly observe among many founders.

It is extremely critical for a business to be able to distribute your product in a cost-effective manner. After achieving a product–market fit and seeing a recurring demand for the service, many founders make the mistake of pumping money into marketing and acquiring users at any cost. That is a recipe for disaster. The best startups solve for Customer Acquisition Cost (CAC) first before launching the rocket ship. If the startup is unable to generate more demand cheaply, the startup will not be able to achieve positive unit economics. That means it will continue to bleed money on every new customer. That model doesn't sustain for long.

For a long time, Mehul struggled with optimizing his marketing budget and finding the best channels to reach his target audience, who are mostly urban professionals looking for a convenient and personalized way to practice yoga. He tried various platforms like Facebook and Google but found them to be a black box as they constantly changed their algorithms and policies. He felt frustrated when he was close to solving the marketing problem but still could not cross the finish line. For him, the finish line is making his business positive at a unit level, i.e. earning more from each customer than what he spent on acquiring them. He found solace and support in talking to other founders who were going through similar struggles. He realized that he was not alone and marketing a new product was not a formula, but a process of trial and error, where he had to test different hypotheses and measure the results. He kept trying and failing fast to find the breakthrough that would make his business sustainable and ready for growth. He says that trying and failing fast is the best practice to deal with the trials of marketing costs. He shares that as an entrepreneur you do not want to run out of money before testing all your ideas that could make a difference.

Stay Afloat!

While Sangeeta had set off on her adventure, for a year, the startup did not earn any revenue. Being bootstrapped meant spending money out of the pocket. Some of the places where Sangeeta needed to be visible were global shows of military aviation, navy or army in Europe or Asia. She dipped into her savings but was cognizant that she needed to start earning soon to be sustainable. She continued to make the effort to create great content and be present wherever the action was. This meant sending her team members to international shows as well.

Sangeeta realized being a media partner in some of the big shows gave her visibility. It started with a media partnership at Undersea Defence Technology (UDT), a global show for submarines in Bremen, Germany. This started a still-continuing series of global media partnerships with air, land systems, naval systems, homeland security and civil aviation shows. It meant and still means investing time, money and emotion into the world of aviation and defence. In entrepreneurship, more than the idea, what matters is showing up, day after day. In October 2016, she received a call from Rolls Royce, one of the largest defence manufacturers, saying that they wanted to advertise on her site. Sangeeta was over the moon, because she had finally broken through.

One of the most critical aspects of success for an entrepreneur is to maintain a positive and consistent cash flow. As advertisements started trickling in organically, Sangeeta made sector-wise marketing plans for advertising. She realized that advertisement plans for small Indian manufacturers would differ from those of international giants. She fondly remembers a story where the National Academy of Legal Studies and Research (NALSAR), a public law school that had a centre for aerospace and defence laws, reached out and wanted to advertise but did not have the budget for the same. Sangeeta politely refused to do it for free but valued the relationship that could be established. Hence, she asked them for Rs 5000, which was the amount to cover the uploading costs, but took nothing more. This investment in the relationship paid off eventually as they became advertisers at a later stage.

Cash flow is maintained like the flow of a river. It starts slowly but drop by drop, catches pace. Though many advertisers invested in monthly plans only, a mighty river was in the making. Sangeeta also allowed university students in aerospace and defence to showcase their projects on the website, further building networks that would nurture the startup for the future.

It is an assumption that one needs to be young, have a finance background and/or have access to strong social circles to run a startup. A lot of founders feel stressed about keeping afloat. But what Sangeeta showed was that you don't need a certain age, background or gender to be financially savvy.

Be True to Yourself

Samarth left his cushy job as an engineer to pursue his dream of making films. He loved documentaries and wanted to tell stories that mattered. He made his first film, *The Unreserved*, which got him a National Award. But awards don't pay the bills, and Samarth soon realized how hard it was to make a living as an independent filmmaker. Being an IITian, he had no contacts in the film industry.

He gave up on filmmaking and decided to go back to school. He enrolled in a liberal arts course at Ashoka University and thought about becoming a peace activist. He even considered applying to Harvard Divinity School. He convinced himself that filmmaking could not be a career.

But fate had other plans. At an alumni event, he met a film producer who had seen *The Unreserved* and loved it. She offered him a chance to direct a film that she would finance. Samarth was stunned. He felt a surge of excitement and passion that he had not felt in a long time. He forgot all about his academic plans and agreed to take the offer, on the spot.

He chose filmmaking again, knowing the risks and challenges. He knew he might not make much money or get much recognition, but he also knew he loved making films more than anything else. When the pandemic hit and the film industry came to a halt, he could not afford living out of Mumbai and had to move to Gurdaspur. But he did not regret his decision. He was happy to follow his passion, even if it meant facing more trials with money.

Contentment Is the Path to Bliss

In 2008, when the global financial crisis hit hard, markets were dry, and redBus was struggling to survive. They had no money left to pay their employees, and they had to accept a lower valuation from an investor to raise some funds. This is when Phani made a mental note as the CEO. He vowed to never let this happen again and to always grab any opportunity to raise capital, even if they didn't need it.

Four years later, in 2012, redBus was doing much better. They were profitable and growing fast. They had received a huge term sheet from a venture capitalist who wanted to invest in them. Phani saw this as a chance to make up for the past losses and to secure their future. He decided to create a bidding war among the investors. Soon enough, they had eight more term sheets from different firms. One of them was from Naspers, a South African media giant that had a presence in India.

One of their existing investors, who had been with them for seven years, wanted to exit by selling their shares to the new investors. This is called a secondary sale. But Naspers came up with a different idea. They offered to buy out the entire company, including all the shares of the founders and the employees.

Phani was stunned by this offer. He had never thought of selling his company before. He loved redBus and he was proud of what they had built. But he also knew that running a startup was not easy. The last eight years had been stressful and exhausting. He had seen one of his co-founders leave the company. He had also received resignation letters from his senior managers and co-founders at least five times during the journey.

Phani wondered what he would do if he sold redBus. He could become financially independent and pursue other interests. He could go to Stanford to study. He could live many lives in this one life, if he left. He could also miss out on the potential growth and impact of redBus if he stayed.

Phani chose contentment over greed. He agreed to sell redBus to Naspers for over $100 million, making it one of the biggest acquisitions in India's startup history. He felt happy and relieved, but also sad and nostalgic.

He had fulfilled his dream of becoming an entrepreneur, but he also realized that it was time to move on and start a new chapter in his life.

Trials and Temptations of Risk Management

Managing risk is an inherent part of entrepreneurship, but it can also be a source of temptation. Entrepreneurs must weigh the pros and cons of every decision they make and be prepared for the

consequences. They have to take calculated risks that align with
their vision and goals.

Through the journey, one can never have a one-trick pony approach to problem-solving. The amount of risk involved in a particular stage will have to be balanced with caution and the founder is challenged to have a strategic mindset that is agile and alive to the journey.

The psychology of risk perception is often influenced by past experiences, inherent personality traits and cognitive biases. This subjective assessment makes the ability to be successful in a venture unpredictable and hence, there is no single formula. Being self-aware and understanding the inherent factors in managing risk can help entrepreneurs make informed decisions, navigate uncertainty and increase the likelihood of success.

Expect the Unexpected!

Mayank was now wholly committed to transforming the lives of farmers in Gaya and improving the food chain. He was passionate about his mission and ready to face any challenges. He started by working closely with the local community to understand their problems. He spent hours talking to the farmers, visiting their fields, learning about their crops and practices. He discovered that tuberculosis was a major health issue that affected many people and caused them to be ostracized from society. The government provided medicines, but they also required rich nutrition to counteract the side effects, which was not available to the locals. Most of them survived on rice and lentils, which did not provide enough vitamins and minerals. Mayank and his team decided to solve this problem by growing three crops—moringa, palm and pumpkin—that could provide the necessary nutrition to the affected patients. Moringa was a superfood that had many health benefits, palm was a source of oil and sugar and pumpkin was a versatile vegetable that could be used in many dishes. These crops were suitable for the climate and soil of Gaya and required minimal investment and risk. The idea was brilliant, and the team executed it flawlessly. The locals were enthusiastic about the project and hoped to benefit from it in terms of health, income and dignity. They chose to start with pumpkin as their first crop.

But then disaster struck. In July 2016, Gaya experienced floods after forty years. All the saplings were destroyed. Almost three or four years of crops were lost. The community lost faith in Mayank and his team and blamed them for their loss. It was a huge setback for the young venture, right in its first year. It showed how unpredictable and cruel nature can be, and how one has to be prepared for the worst even when doing good work. Mayank was facing a critical test of his resilience and determination as an entrepreneur. His survival depended on how he would overcome this crisis.

Exercise

1. Draft a plan of action in this case, if you were Mayank.
2. Draft a one-pager on one near-death experience that your startup has faced (if any). What could be done differently to avoid it?

Victory Must Be Earned—Over and Over Again

Having raised a million dollars through business plan competitions, Dharamveer and his band of cowboy entrepreneurs were ready to take on the world. As he had planned, DV had started Zostel on his own terms—in an industry of choice, with people of choice. He could wear his shorts when he wanted at work as the CEO, and had the funding that he needed to get going. Sounds like a fairytale, doesn't it? Sounds like it is going to be an easy ride into the unicorn club. But was it?

If you are following our visionary entrepreneur, by now, you would know that all he wanted to do was play all day. Zostel was about bringing that same attitude to revolutionizing the way hospitality works in India. As DV mentions, he came into work with his core team with an attitude to win and smash it out of the park every single day. With wisdom beyond his years, he shares that entrepreneurship is a way to find yourself, in the sense that you will express who you are through the startup. But the question is what you believe to be true—how true can YOU be to it? This will be continually tested throughout your journey. If there is a contradiction between what you think, say and do, the only person at the end of the day who will live with that is you.

DV had already said no to placements, CV creation sessions and all the steps a college demands of you to get a job and follow the rat race. He promised his colleagues that he will not take a job and give his all to Zostel. While talking to us, he shared that people who have an entrepreneurial mindset don't wait around for something to happen. They just show up and get started and so, he got started.

For DV, Zostel was not just a startup but an interesting experiment. However, he was unaware of two variables—the market size and how fast they could scale. Both were blind spots. Given that it was a brick-and-mortar business, venture capitalists were not too excited about investing heavily upfront. Even without the need for capital, setting up a unique hostel chain in various parts of the country would bring its own challenges.

The concept of travel in young Indians was evolving, with the great Indian middle class rising and disposable income now available to young people. Add to this improved transportation infrastructure and a desire to seek cultural and natural identity for not just the country, but for the youth themselves. As the country was becoming self-sufficient, there was a need for young people to seek out offbeat destinations that were authentic. Through this, they could get away from their families and societies for a while or longer and seek who they were in their own space. Zostel was catering to that.

Add to this the digital influence on the market. Between 2013 and 2015, the number of smartphone users in India grew four times to twenty-five crore. With smartphones in the hands of a large part of the population, travel planning could be done with information, insights and options. Due to this, technology would be the differentiator. DV had built a strong team of talented people with tech backgrounds from premier colleges, who built their own proprietary software that gave the edge to a youth hostel chain in a market that was not there yet. In a business where margins were small, big data and tech helped gain 15–20 per cent on top line and influenced the entire bottom line to create value for Zostel. DV coached, mentored and learned from the core team who were not afraid of conversations, their own capabilities and achieving a bold vision. He smiles as he fondly remembers the culture of innovation and victorious energies that they had co-created.

Everything seemed to be going well. The core team saw an opportunity in expanding the business to a budget hotel aggregator chain and voila, Zo Rooms was born. It operated as an online platform that aimed to provide standardized and affordable accommodation options to travellers across various cities in India. They aimed to differentiate themselves in the highly competitive hospitality industry by offering competitive pricing, standardized amenities and a tech-led, seamless booking experience, which they had already built for Zostel.

Zo Rooms scaled rapidly and secured over $30 million funding from investors. The venture aggressively expanded its operations, increasing its presence in multiple cities across India and rapidly scaling its partner network. As the competition with its closest rival heated up, it received an offer for a merger. DV and his core team were happy as this would allow his founding team to be paid off for their efforts. This sounded like a fairytale but after a few months, the deal fell through, and the matter is still in court.

As DV reflects on the saga, he goes back to his core motivation of playing. He shares how, if you play, you need to go ALL IN to be able to win or lose. Winning is fine but for failing, it has to be earned, and you only earn failure when you are fully committed to your venture. A lot of people want to fake the learning from a half attempt, but that way, they are not evolving in the true sense. It is like Batman being stuck in the well, unable to get out and the only way to overcome the chasm was jumping without the rope in the *Dark Knight Rises*, adds DV. He shares how it has been an emotional rollercoaster to go through this journey, but the starting point was dreaming a bold dream and seeing where he landed—and he does not regret any of it.

DV was twenty-six and one of the hardest things he has done is shut down Zo Rooms. He shared how it is easier to start a company than shut one down! Despite the turmoil and departure of a good team and the world telling him how he could have done things differently, DV survived this challenge. He shares how one should not be biased about the outcome and reflect objectively on what the learnings were. He shared how whenever he got stuck, he changed his environment.

This time, he packed his bags and decided to go to a friend who was working in Silicon Valley in the US. After letting the disappointment of the last few months sink in, he used the time to self-reflect on improving his stance towards challenges and started meeting people around him. He even went to Burning Man, an annual community event that happens in the Black Rock Desert of Nevada, USA. It is known for its unique and vibrant culture, artistic expression and emphasis on communal participation—just the stimulation DV needed. While he was there, he took his time to contemplate what he wanted to achieve and shared how it is time that shows you what you would have missed in the heat of action. He did smaller things like making a website end to end, doing simple things to remind himself of what he could still do. To walk a few tiny steps after an accident—these were steps of self-determination and starting again.

There, all by himself, he looked at the past, present and future and envisioned a Trillion Dollar Company. Another bold dream!

Risk of Burnout Is Real

When you are driven by purpose, at times you start doing more things than humanly possible. Everything seems like an opportunity. And many of those things then start leading to lower return on investments. Not just that, it can start leading to you burning out.

Nihal was expanding Limitless in all directions. He was building products, designing programmes and conducting workshops across the world. It was great for him initially, because it was truly exercising his creativity. But reality strikes hard when you know you have bills and salaries to pay. There is a conflict between the creative spirit and practicality of things. And that starts to bring stress.

Eventually, he had to let go of too much novelty and bring back focus on to the hero products. He still builds blueprints for fun, to keep the creative spirit alive but does not take it forward unless there is a path to revenue.

He was also living across three countries: Canada, Germany and India. Since 2021, he spent more than two months in a single place. It was physically and mentally exhausting. It's hard to build and maintain deeper relationships when you are always living out of suitcases. And the lack of permanent space can also burn you out. Nihal shares that it has been difficult for him to let go of anchors in life, to let go of the comfort that a traditional lifestyle brings.

To overcome burnouts, Nihal has built the following structure:

a. **Antidote:** One needs to rest in a way that is a complete reciprocal of what keeps you busy. Since he is in the space of education and knowledge, Nihal is soaking up as much information as possible every day by consuming content, listening to podcasts and talking to people. So, rest for him cannot be reading.

b. **Have an official cheerleader:** Someone who you can call up anytime and who will make you feel good about yourself and life. Someone you know will make you laugh.

c. **Have a brain trust**: In his case, Nihal has a community of single founders who connect regularly. They talk about their struggles as well as share ideas and resources to deal with them. He has collaborated with each of them on certain projects, thereby having an interim co-founder for a few months.

d. **Create a list of needs:** This is part of his self-care routine. Nihal has listed items that his body and mind need related to fun, connection, intimacy and humour. He has a ritual where he goes through the list every Sunday. All of us have weeks that just feel off, as if something is wrong but we don't know what. But when he goes through the list, invariably something pops up. E.g.: This week I crave connection or calmness. The next steps become easier after that.

Exercise

1. Write two ways of resting, which are completely an antidote to your daily work routine.

2. Ask someone to be an official cheerleader for you. Mention to them why you need it, and what you expect them to do and not do.

3. Create a brain trust of five people who are having a similar journey as yours. Create a structure to connect regularly with them.

4. Create a list of needs. Search on the web on what are the various needs humans have. Write the ones

that you think you have (edit it every year). Fix a time for every Sunday to go through the list. Do this for ten weeks. Log your experience.

Trials and Temptations of Encountering Biases

Entrepreneurs often face biases that negatively impact organizational culture, morale and productivity. This could lead to not just heartburn for the impacted individuals, but lead to attrition, impact on mental health and even legal issues. Overcoming such biases would often mean challenging the status quo and overcoming resistance to foster a culture of inclusion.

Won't Earn Less than My Wife!

Nitin's company wanted to hire a head of technology. It was the most coveted role in the company, which was working on artificial intelligence.

They had been searching for months, but no one seemed to fit the bill. The candidates were either too inexperienced, too arrogant or too demanding. Nitin was losing hope and patience. He wondered if he would ever find the right person for the job.

Then one day, he received an email from his recruiter. There was a candidate who had aced all the technical rounds and was eager to meet the founders. Nitin was intrigued. He checked the candidate's resume and was impressed by his credentials. He had worked for some of the top tech companies in the country and had a proven track record of delivering successful projects. Nitin decided to give him a chance.

He scheduled a final interview with the candidate, along with his co-founders. The interview was supposed to be a cultural fit round, where they would assess the candidate's personality, values and motivation. Nitin expected it to be a smooth and pleasant conversation.

But he was wrong.

As soon as they started talking about the compensation, the candidate dropped a bombshell. He demanded a 50 per cent hike from his previous salary. Nitin and his co-founders were shocked. They asked him why he wanted such a huge increase. The candidate replied that his wife had recently got promoted at her job and that he wanted to earn more than her so that he could keep his head high at home.

Nitin and his co-founders were speechless. They couldn't believe what they were hearing. They realized that the candidate had a sexist and insecure mindset that did not align with their culture of meritocracy, equality and respect. They knew that hiring him would be a disaster for their team and their company.

They decided to reject him on the spot.

They thanked him for his time and politely told him that they were looking for someone who valued performance over ego, who respected women as equals.

The candidate was stunned. He couldn't believe that he had lost the opportunity.

Nitin and his co-founders breathed a sigh of relief. They knew that they had to keep looking for their ideal head of technology, without compromising on the culture. As founders, there is always a choice to be made between culture and short-term gains. Most often, founders chose short-term gains while parking culture for a later date. This is a recipe for disaster.

The Shadow of Bias

If you look at the job description for any job in the world, you will notice what is omnipresent are soft skills. Skills like stakeholder management, communicating effectively, resilience, conflict management and patience separate a good candidate from a great candidate. In the traditional family setup, women grow up polishing these soft skills, whether they are daughters-in-law, mothers or sisters.

Sangeeta Saxena is a female journalist in a male-dominated bastion of armed forces journalism. She took a break for family and so, when she is out in the field, she has her college juniors at higher posts. She faced resistance as editors took female journalists with a pinch of salt. Even though her media house sent her abroad for a show, they went with a story written by a male journalist, who was writing it from his home. 'We have run out of space,' was the excuse she was given.

But this discrimination is not recent. It has always been there. Sangeeta was a gold medalist from Pune University and landed herself an internship with a famous newspaper. She was a hard-working intern and found out about a new rifle the Defence Research and Development Organisation (DRDO) was making. The editor tasked her to get the details from Delhi and Sangeeta set about using her networks to get the story. On her persistence, DRDO sent a letter inviting Sangeeta to see the prototype of the rifle. Elated, Sangeeta ran with the letter to the editor's office, only to be confounded by his rage. The editor was furious that the invitation was in her name and not in the name of a senior journalist like him. He instructed her to get the name changed but DRDO refused. Finally, the story did not happen.

Sangeeta shares how she has to work ten times harder to prove herself every day in an industry surrounded by men, which means she has to write content with depth and meaning and at scale. She shared how by creating content consistently, she has been able to build credibility, but gender bias and stereotypes still shadow the skills, abilities and leadership potential of all women in all fields.

We spoke to women entrepreneurs across industries ranging from media, technology, filmmaking and so on. These were entrepreneurs of various age groups (thirties to fifties) and from metros as well as smaller towns. A common theme a lot of them spoke about was feeling like imposters. Imposter syndrome refers to the feeling of inadequacy and self-doubt despite evidence of competence. Women often experience imposter syndrome, which can undermine their confidence and hold them back from pursuing ambitious goals or taking on leadership roles.

* * *

Trials and temptations define the entrepreneur. At this stage, obstacles and barriers must be surpassed and this is where the faith in 'call to adventure' or the counsel of a mentor come in handy. One must move into this stage with resilience, where our hero must battle the demons, external and internal, to move ahead in his or her journey. This stage questions, forces the entrepreneur to choose and there is the suspense of whether they will make it through. The last self of the entrepreneur often dies metaphorically as they battle these demons, but from the ashes, rises the transformed hero, wiser and evolved.

Exercise

Set an alarm for 3 minutes, close your eyes and start observing your breath. Thoughts will come but gently push them away like a boat in water. Bring your attention back to your breath. Focus on your breath but do not regulate it. Once the alarm rings, gently open your eyes and now, start thinking about the problem at hand. You will be able to see it with more clarity.

Chapter 6

Transformation and Return

'The privilege of a lifetime is to become who you truly are.'

—Joseph Campbell

After enduring countless trials and temptations, our heroes find themselves far removed from the comforts of home, which now feel like a distant memory. Along the way, they have faced both external and internal battles—fighting enemies, confronting fears and overcoming their own weaknesses. Scarred and weary, they stand at a pivotal moment where they are faced with a profound realization.

This is the stage where the hero undergoes a symbolic death—not physical, but a deep internal transformation. It signifies the end of their old self; letting go of limiting beliefs, habits, fears and doubts that shaped their worldview.

The hero realizes that it was these outdated ways of thinking and living that held them back all along.

As the old self dies, a new version of the hero emerges—one that is spiritually and psychologically reborn with a deeper sense of purpose. They understand that this journey is not just about external achievements, but also an inner awakening. By surrendering to their destiny, the hero embraces change as necessary and inevitable. They embrace this transformation, knowing that in order to move forward, they must let go of the past and step into the unknown future as their most authentic self.

At this stage, the hero transforms from a mere survivor to an empowered individual—ready to face the final challenges with renewed strength, clarity and wisdom.

This is not easy. It makes our hero confront their deepest fears, insecurities and limitations. The hero can now clearly see all that hinders their growth and relinquishes the attachments, ego and outdated beliefs holding them back. This juncture is also the stepping stone to a profound internal transformation, akin to the transformation of a caterpillar to a butterfly, which although painful and slow, is a magnificent journey of rebirth.

With the transformation comes wisdom, and the hero seeks reconciliation, resolves past conflicts, makes amends and starts coming to terms with their own character. Psychologically, these characteristics, positive or negative, might be hidden and are only brought to the surface by going through the trials. By now, the hero reconciles these hidden characteristics and emerges with a sense of purpose and clarity, ready to evolve into the next phase of their journey.

Burning Man

As Dharamveer returned to India, he came back a transformed individual. One of the unique elements of the Burning Man festival is that at the end of the event, a huge wooden effigy of a man is burnt. There are many versions of what significance this holds but in the context of this book, we would like to believe it signifies the death of the earlier self of the hero. Having gone through trials and temptations, the hero, being in that focal point of time, space and energy, ceases to exist in terms of past aspirations. Having shut down Zo Rooms, it was the death of a part of DV's venture and with it, a version of him. DV admits he returned with clarity and the DV who was naive and emotionally volatile had died with the Burning Man.

With this death came realization and wisdom. And now it was time to re-focus on the core adventure—

Zostel. From his experiences, it dawned on DV that the actual treasure is not securing funding or profitability or scaling fast. It was what had brought humanity so far—community!

When early humans were fighting sabre-tooth tigers and the ravages of nature, what differentiated them from other far superior animals was their ability to come together. Around a fire, narrating their stories, they found common ground and set out to achieve the impossible. The same sense of community is what is the differentiator for any hospitality brand today. To have a loyal set of individuals who come together to create anything.

Zostel renewed its focus on affordable, comfortable and social lodging experiences, catering to the needs of budget-conscious travellers looking to explore India on a budget. DV scaled Zostel to over eighty properties. He shares that his grandfather advised him that smart people learn from their mistakes, but the smartest people learn from others' mistakes. Instead of onboarding big VCs that would then have a say in the running of Zostel and dilute the vision, DV and team chose to expand on a franchise model. He connected with local entrepreneurs who wanted to partner to create unique experiences, whether it was Jibhi in Himachal Pradesh or Pokhara in Nepal. They organized events, workshops and activities at their hostels to encourage interaction and cultural exchange among guests. Travellers who visited Zostels and tourists who visited India started following the trail of Zostels in their travels across India.

Throughout its journey, Zostel continued to innovate and incorporate technology into its operations. They launched a user-friendly mobile app and implemented various digital solutions to enhance the overall guest experience, making it a differentiator in the competitive market.

DV started focusing on amplifying the power of human connection and communities. He was conscious in choosing organic growth over the steroids given by investor funding. What this meant was that it would require time and patience. The time invested would create self-sustaining communities that would set roots and grow the network of Zostels into the thriving business it is today.

Today, DV is all about quality AND quantity rather than speed and scale. He always believed that if you are not taking a step forward, you are taking a step backward, but now that step is a measured one, based on wisdom and self-awareness. From building fast, he now wants to build something that will stay on forever and leave a legacy. That is a fundamental mind shift for the new DV!

The Train Back Home

A shy and quiet boy caught a train from the railway station in Ghatshila in Jharkhand to his college, IIT Kharagpur in West Bengal. He did not know what his future would bring. Having started the journey under the weight of financial difficulties, living with his relatives to complete his school education, and with the aim of somehow getting a well-paying job, he joined the best engineering institution in the country.

At IIT Kharagpur, while he was finishing his course, he also contributed to extracurricular activities of making an impact in the villages around Kharagpur. He helped NGOs raise funds and conduct events, thereby gaining organizational skills.

At the end of his college tenure, he did get a dream corporate job, worked hard and paid off his financial dues. He then left the job and followed his heart to work on social innovation, creating impact on the ground. He faced a dilemma in terms of the people he worked with, ethics, the opportunity cost of not doing a plush corporate job and the friction of bureaucracy in India. The journey of an entrepreneur made him take the responsibility of his team, working with co-founders and planning to disrupt the development sector in India.

He shared how with time, he evolved into becoming accepting of people and situations. From a person who was often discontented, he is far more at peace with himself now. From being shy, fearful and low in confidence, he is now a confident and calm person, who believes he can bring about change if he sets himself to it. Like Shah Rukh Khan in *Swades*[4], he has found his bulb moment and is lighting up the lives of people in India who need it.

What sets Ankit apart from other entrepreneurs is that he planned his life despite all odds. Even though he did not have the financial cushion to get into social sector entrepreneurship, he spent the time creating it before getting down to pursuing his dreams of making a difference. Ankit remained persistent, envisioning the day he would return to Ghatshila—to the very place where his journey began—to give back in a way that could truly impact the community. He saw himself stepping back into

---

4 *Swades*, directed by Ashutosh Gowariker (Mumbai: UTV Motion Pictures, 2004), featuring Shah Rukh Khan.

that familiar train station, transformed and ready to make a difference. And he is only getting started . . .

Homecoming

What is life without a sense of meaning? Without a sense of purpose? Whether you are starting your journey or are already a celebrity, purpose is what drives you forward. Without it, you feel lost and stuck. Samarth had already won a National Award for his documentary, *The Unreserved*. After that, he poured his heart and soul into his documentary *Borderlands*, a project that was more than just a film for him. It was a tribute to his hometown and the people who lived at the borders, who are often rendered invisible as the narrative of war and violence takes precedence in the public eye. He had spent more than three years working on it, travelling, interviewing, filming, editing and hoping that his work would make a difference. He had won a National Award for *The Unreserved*, and he was confident that *Borderlands* would be even better for his career.

But life had other plans for him. The pandemic hit the world hard, and the film industry was no exception. The market for independent documentaries dried up, and Samarth struggled to find a buyer for his film. He got feedback from traditional distributors that they have simply travelled the country and stitched together a few interviews. Samarth started feeling that *'Humne toh shayad film bhi nahi banayi hai* [perhaps we have not really made a film].' He had invested all his savings and energy into this venture, and he had no backup plan. He had to leave Mumbai, the City of Dreams, and move back to his hometown, where he felt like an outsider. He had no friends or colleagues who understood his passion for filmmaking. He felt isolated and hopeless. He had lost his purpose in life.

Samarth tried to distract himself with other things, but nothing could fill the void in his heart. He missed his film community, his creative outlet, his sense of achievement. He wondered if he had made a mistake by pursuing his dream. He wondered if he would ever get another chance to make a film. He wondered if he would ever find meaning in his life again.

But Samarth persisted. Films were like his art and if artists don't put their art out there, who will? Nine out of ten films get rejected at the first stage of application to any film festival. But Samarth did not give up. Every time Netflix would reject him, and every time that there would be a new leader who would join Netflix, Samarth would go and pitch. He would simply 'be at it'. Eventually, *Borderlands* won Samarth his second National Film Award.

Coming from a border town himself, Samarth had covered his mother's story as well in *Borderlands*, in addition to other stories of people who live at the borders. The story is extremely personal to Samarth and has deeply affected his personal relationship with his mother. Having faced a bottled-up childhood with a single rat race agenda, he used to feel suffocated staying at home for even a day. With *Borderlands*, he got connected with his family at a human level. This was a huge transformation for him. His parents threw a party for the whole town to celebrate his success with *Borderlands*. He stayed for over a year this time at his home! Truly a homecoming!

For the first twenty years of his life, Samarth was running blindly. Then he moved from engineering to filmmaking. For the next ten years, he was trying to find his feet. Moments of doubt led him to explore running an education startup, be a teacher and even explore divinity. But he persisted with his passion. Today, when he sits in the train from his hometown Dinanagar, he knows where he is heading. He knows his tribe, his place. He is one with himself.

And yes, a mechanical engineer can become a successful filmmaker!

The Fairytale

In 2013, Phani, at the age of thirty-three, had sold his first company and a piece of his heart, redBus. It was not an easy decision as redBus was making Rs 2 crore in profits already on sales of over Rs 600 crore. If an Internet marketplace is making profits like that, it would take a lot for it to fail from here on. There are strong network effects—more sellers mean more selection, which can attract more customers, and more customers means more business opportunities for new sellers. However, he and his co-founders were jaded with the seven years they had poured into building the biggest online portal for transportation in India.

Phani decided to take the deal on the table as he shares that an entrepreneur should know where to stop. Life is a marathon, not a sprint; founders often don't know how to balance priorities.

He agrees one should push the envelope in the growth stage when it comes to market share, revenues, etc., but in some areas like legal issues, mental health boundaries and more, one should know where to draw the line.

After exiting redBus, Phani was being advised that these are his prime years. Why doesn't he jump into his next venture like everyone else? Phani thought that if he starts his next cycle of entrepreneurship now, by the time he exits, he would be fifty, because startups take over fifteen years. This is also a time when he was blessed with his first child. It dawned on him that he had an opportunity to be free and that it was he who had to make the choice.

And he made the choice that entrepreneurs very rarely do today. In his prime, he went to Stanford to study social psychology, art and design. He chose to be a full-time father to his first child. He chose to go deeper into sustainability and opened his own foundation. His family was shocked and shared their concerns on how at a young age, he started giving his money away to charity. But Phani knew what he was doing. He realized he had enough money to be content.

Contentment—what a powerful thought in a world that is constantly asking for bigger, better, faster. Phani is a breath of fresh air in the world that constantly puts pressure to keep performing and being featured in Forbes 30 Under 30 lists. He demonstrated a deliberate intent to slow down and savour his success. From being an aggressive CEO, who gave an employee a piece of his mind if he did not like something as minute as the colour of the buttons on their app, to being a fulfilled entrepreneur, Phani had completed his journey of transformation.

* * *

Transformation is not a superficial change that you can simply think your way into. It is a fundamental shift only possible if you are willing to take risks and put yourself in positions that will bring about a profound change in who you are. It will resolve the contradictions in your thought, words and actions.

The transformation in the heroes is driven by challenges, experience and self-discovery that come with starting and running a business. Personal transformation is crucial to the evolution of an entrepreneur, contributing to their success and fulfillment. All entrepreneurs who go through this phase experience heightened self-awareness and emotional intelligence. This is the phase where it all starts to make sense and sets them up for a grand comeback.

Exercise

Pick up a journal. Set a time period for self-reflection every week. Answer these questions: What were the key challenges I faced? How did I respond to them? What were the emotions I felt through the process? What did I do differently? Finally, express gratitude for the people, experiences or circumstances that helped you learn. Do it for ten weeks.

The success of an entrepreneurial venture hinges on numerous factors—product–market fit, market conditions, timing and more. Yet, amidst all these external influences, one factor remains unquestionably decisive in shaping the journey of a startup: the evolution of the entrepreneur. No matter how grand or humble the beginning may be, what ultimately distinguishes successful startups from the many that struggle or fail is not just the idea, market conditions or resources, but the personal transformation of their founders.

Throughout this book, we've explored stories where startups have experienced a wide range of outcomes—some have been acquired, others have merged, a few have shut down and many are still striving for that breakthrough moment. But what is consistent across all these stories is that the founders, the heroes of our entrepreneurial narrative, are no longer the same people who set out at the start of their journey. They answered the call to adventure and were transformed by it. The challenges, setbacks, triumphs and lessons they encountered along the way have fundamentally reshaped who they are.

At this point in their journey, they carry with them a precious boon—the wisdom gained from their trials and experiences. This boon is more than just knowledge of business strategies or market tactics; it is a deep, internal understanding of themselves, their resilience, their capabilities and their purpose. The battlefields of entrepreneurship, filled with sleepless nights, failures, pivots and rare victories, have left their mark on the hero. And now, as the dust settles, the hero may look back nostalgically at the action, but there is a sense of peace in having completed this phase of the adventure.

This moment signifies the return—the hero's homecoming. Just as Bilbo returns to the Shire after his adventures, and Harry Potter returns to Hogwarts after confronting great trials, these entrepreneurs, too, return to their 'mundane' world. But they are forever changed. They re-enter their communities not as the wide-eyed dreamers who left, but as wise leaders, equipped with hard-earned insights. They have transcended the limitations and fears that once held them back and are now able to share their wisdom with others.

Many of these founders, having undergone their transformation, now embrace the role of mentors, guides and coaches. They understand that the entrepreneurial journey is not just about personal success, but also about uplifting others, inspiring positive change and helping the next generation of innovators along their path.

As they return to this new normal, what the heroes leave behind are the doubts, fears and constraints that marked the beginning of their journey. Their perspective is now broadened, and they are equipped with the emotional resilience and greater understanding needed to face whatever new horizons lie ahead. Their evolution is complete, yet the adventure continues in a new form as they return to the world they left behind—but now with the strength and wisdom to shape it in meaningful ways.

Now, it is time to walk alongside our heroes and witness how they return not only to the world but to the purpose and destiny that has been forged by their journey.

Conquer the World with Home and Heart

As Dharamveer now thinks back on his journey, he reflects that while he is the CEO of a successful startup, he acknowledges it is now time to go home with all the wisdom and experiences he has gained through the journey.

When he set out to start Zostel, DV did not see it as just another startup that he started as a hobby so that he could exit, earn some quick money and live a comfortable life. Coming from a middle-class Indian family, he saw how young India had this energy of wanting to express themselves, free from the confines of societal pressures, but hardly found the space to do so.

Biswapati, another startup founder we spoke to, shares how every young Indian has encountered toxic uncles and aunties who, instead of encouraging girls and boys to follow their heart, discourage them to take up conventional paths of education and professions and advise their parents to rein them in.

DV says that Zostel is about giving such *dreamers* that starting point. They have created a social environment where ideas come together, and youngsters can create whatever they want. DV wants to give back to young India something he always believed in: 'Follow your heart.'

DV continues to build Zostels in every part of the country, giving dreamers a space to express themselves. He also shares how all the incredible individuals he met and worked with while building Zostel are now all startup founders or part of the leadership team of startups. He is happy that he was a part of the magic that existed and identified the potential of this founder universe.

Talking about following the heart, DV is now back where it all started. He left Jodhpur when he was fourteen. He shares how in the period of the last fifteen or sixteen years, he has travelled many countries, built companies worth millions, killed himself and been reborn. DV used to visit Jodhpur on holidays or vacations for a while, but visited cities like Varanasi, Kolkata or Bengaluru right after that. He regrets not spending more time with his family and being there for them, helping them. This is a thought not just for himself, but something all entrepreneurs could consider on the price one pays for the journey.

Over the years, having been exposed to the world now, he appreciates capitalism and how the world goes round. He recognizes its role in driving economic growth, fostering innovation and providing individuals with opportunities for entrepreneurship and wealth creation, while also acknowledging its challenges and inequalities. And with that, he appreciates his home, Jodhpur, even more. Whenever he needs to visit, he can visit Dubai, Silicon Valley or New York. But increasingly now, DV feels he knows what is there to know and there are no blind spots if one stays vigilant in today's connected world. The imposter syndrome is long gone, and the FOMO has given way to well-earned self-assurance. If you are young and willing to learn, you challenge yourself and don't follow the beaten path—and you will most likely get there.

As DV reflects on his incredible journey, he sees that this is just the beginning of a much larger adventure—a journey not just for him, but for all of humanity. From a small-town dreamer to the creator of a global community, he's built more than just startups; he's built movements and spaces where people can truly live and connect. His vision for Zo World is a bold one: a world where technology and community unite to lead the next generation through the chaos of our times, with love, creativity and endless possibilities.

We are entering an age of abundance, where human potential is limitless. In this twenty-first century, we have the power to evolve from mere monkeys chasing survival to superhumans creating our destiny. Our mission as a species is no longer just to survive but to thrive—to experience, to explore, and yes, to party! Life is the greatest adventure, and it's meant to be celebrated.

With Zo World, DV is crafting a global network of Zostels, Zo Houses and Zo Nodes, with citizens of the Zo World transforming living and travelling as a celebration of life itself. Every corner of the world is being unlocked, not just as destinations but as places of human connection and discovery. This is humanity's mission: to come together, break down barriers and create a world where we are free to be ourselves and follow our hearts.

There Is No Age or Gender for Entrepreneurship

Why don't we play a game of 'two lies and a truth'. Here they are:

1. Entrepreneurs can be successful only if they start before thirty.
2. Entrepreneurs who are women need to be in certain fields to be successful.
3. Women entrepreneurs are driven and capable, shaped by their experiences overcoming entry barriers, limited opportunities and discrimination.

Well, you are right. There is no age, gender or personality that is a pre-requisite for the journey to begin.

Sangeeta, defence journalist-turned-entrepreneur and a mother of two, reflects on her journey. Having started her entrepreneurship journey in her fifties after her responsibilities had waned, she shares that what is critical to success for an entrepreneur is resilience, persistence, embracing failure, time management and discipline. Women in India develop these skills through the various hoops society makes you jump. Whether being married in a conservative setup or balancing family responsibilities with work or managing children while focusing on a career, competing in a male-dominated world, women are shaped into individuals most suited for entrepreneurship. They learn time management, conflict resolution and most importantly, resilience, through their life experiences.

It is not about whether you were given an opportunity or not. It is about the story you tell yourself. A founder in their thirties, forties, fifties or sixties will have their own unique journey and story to tell. The question is whether you are going to go forth and say a hearty yes to the adventure yet to come. Having said yes and now being a founder of one of the top defence journalism startups, Sangeeta shares how the journey has changed her.

Sangeeta has ceased to exist and ADU has come alive. This is a common theme we find with many startup founders, who have expressed how by the end of their startup journey, they have let go of who they thought they were. Sangeeta shares how the journey often involves encountering numerous challenges, setbacks and failures. These experiences can humble entrepreneurs by reminding them that success is not guaranteed and that there is always room for improvement. Dealing with failures can help entrepreneurs recognize their own limitations and the need to learn and grow from their mistakes. Founders need to be open to receiving constructive feedback from customers, employees and stakeholders. Being receptive to criticism and using it to make improvements demonstrates a willingness to admit shortcomings and a commitment to continuous growth.

Having the capacity to be humble and re-learn all this in your fifties lets Sangeeta's story shatter the idea of who can be an entrepreneur. It is a lesson for a lot of people doubting their potential to start something of their own based on age or gender. It is also a mirror to all those aggressive founders, who feel entrepreneurs need to be from IITs or IIMs in their thirties. Fulfilling her familial obligations in a conservative society, working with people half her age to compete in a male-dominated society or flying in and out of countries to be at the forefront of defence news, Sangeeta did not once regret her entrepreneurial venture. She is now financially independent, her own boss, travelling to shows across the world—she's a name to reckon with in her field.

Today, looking back, she is proud of how far she has come and looks forward to inspiring many more women to break glass ceilings, one bias at a time.

I Am an Imposter No Longer

At the age of sixteen, Devashish cleared the entrance of the National Defence Academy with AIR 1. He joined the army. For the world, his identity was that of army personnel. But just because you crack an entrance exam doesn't mean you are built for it. Devashish felt people who came from sports backgrounds have what it takes to succeed in the army; not a typical guy whose daily routine would be to go to school, be back, study for exams and go on like this. He felt himself to be a big misfit in the army. He felt like an outsider. Even though for the external world he was performing well, Devashish internally did not feel at peace. He did not feel one with his identity and continued to feel like an imposter, who would soon be discovered and expelled. After four years of training and eight years of work, Devashish became a Major in the army with critical responsibilities. It was at this moment when he started believing that he deserved to be there. He had earned it. The imposter syndrome that was with him for twelve years finally went away.

In 2005, Devashish cracked the CAT exam as a topper with a 100th percentile score. After completing his degree, he started a venture with his colleagues from

IIM Ahmedabad. During the early years, he would make himself believe that he is only an entrepreneur because of his co-founders. Without them, he couldn't be one. He would think that the clients and investors coming in are all because of external factors and not because of his contributions. He couldn't accept his identity of being an entrepreneur. This ran on for almost a decade. And then things turned.

In 2013, as a solo founder, Devashish was looking to pivot his recruitment services business as it was difficult to scale. While making the pivot, he wanted to ensure that the clients were taken care of. He did not just want to tell them to look for new vendors; he wanted to ensure that they found one and completed the handover. Thinking this, he identified a respected service provider and told them that he would want to give all his clients to them. The vendor agreed and offered a 50 per cent revenue share in return. Devashish was surprised. He realized there was a market opportunity for them by simply creating demand for service providers. He pivoted his business to becoming an Uber for recruitment businesses. Later, a market leader in the space made a major investment in their business. At this moment, Devashish finally felt that he was not an imposter and had created genuine value in the market. He is an entrepreneur!

He became one with his identity after a decade. He became at peace with himself, again. He no longer thought: 'I am an imposter!'

Return to Community

Mayur cleared the CFA and was looking to generate wealth in the financial sector. Yet, he felt something was missing in his life. He wanted more than just wealth; he wanted to explore the world and meet new people. He decided to quit his job and start NomadGao, a product that connects remote workers and digital nomads with inspiring co-living and co-working spaces.

He travelled to different countries, learned about different cultures and found a community of like-minded people, who shared his passion for adventure and freedom. He also met his wife, who joined him in his journey of nomadic living. Together, they discovered the joy of minimalism, conscious living and authentic human connection. They realized that success is not measured by how much you have, but by how much you experience life; they have grown together in the process. They used technology as a tool to enhance their lifestyle, not as a distraction or an addiction. They are now planning to spend twelve months in twelve different settings for

NomadGao to challenge themselves, learn new skills and create unforgettable memories.

Mayur is not just a founder, he is the leader of a tribe that believes in living life to the fullest. The finance guy is dead, the nomad is born!

Desh ka Culture, Agriculture

Siddhartha was a prince who gave up his wealth and privilege to become the Buddha. He saw that even people who were wealthy and powerful could not escape suffering, and he began to search for a way to end it. He began to question that if there is so much suffering in society, then are you really rich and fulfilled? After many years, he finally achieved enlightenment under a tree in Bodh Gaya.

Mayank's journey is a humble representation of how we all have our own Buddha's journey. Despite facing tremendous natural and organizational challenges, Mayank was determined. The guy who had left his comfortable life in Delhi and taken a train to Gaya wanted to make life comfortable for numerous people in rural and urban India. He had a vision of providing nutritious and organic food to the urban population, while empowering the rural farmers who grew it.

Over the last decade, he has been able to create significant on-ground impact. He helped set up SumArth Kendra, an open innovation lab for farming spread across one-and-a-half acres. The Kendra became a state-of-the-art centre with over Rs 5 crore in assets today. It has a custom hiring centre, where farmers can rent or borrow tools and equipment. It has a single-stop solution with more than seventy types of agriculture and farming techniques. It has a cold storage facility and a processing and value addition centre, where farmers can store, aggregate, prevent wastage and increase the value of their products. It has a residential centre for seventy-five people, where visitors can stay and learn from the farmers. It also has a food processing cluster, where farmers can add value to their products and increase their incomes.

Mayank also helped farmers become aware of innovative policy interventions that benefited them. He advocated for urban gardening policy, which gave a 50 per cent subsidy from the government to people who wanted to grow food on their terraces or balconies. He promoted mushroom cultivation, starting from scratch and scaling it to 1000 growers with support from the National Bank for Agriculture and Rural Development (Nabard) within three years. Eventually, mushrooms became a focus crop under the One District One Product scheme in Gaya due to the efforts of multiple stakeholders. Mayank pioneered commercializing moringa cultivation in the region, which is a highly nutritious plant that can grow in the rocky terrains of Gaya. Efforts led to Punjab National Bank providing Rs 51,000 loans now for moringa growers on Kisan Credit Cards.

Mayank's organization also worked on Sakhi Lakhpati, a programme for women empowerment and menstrual hygiene. He trained women farmers on various aspects of farming, entrepreneurship, leadership and health. He provided them with access to biodegradable menstrual products (pads and cups) made from banana fiber. He created a platform for them to showcase their products and services to urban consumers. He also formed a farmer-producer organization, which is one of the fastest-grossing FPOs in eastern India.

Mayank has been in synergy with the rural way of life, which is generally slower than urban life, but also more sustainable. He built slowly and laid strong foundations. The interventions appeared discrete at times, but they were all towards the common goal of accessibility, education and empowerment. All his programmes were interlinked/ intertwined and complemented each other. Mayank's journey to Gaya transformed his life and the lives of many others. He became healthier, happier and more fulfilled. He created an impact that was beyond his imagination. Mayank is truly an embodiment of the motto: Desh ka culture, agriculture.

I Don't Want My Company to Grow Beyond a Certain Size

After leaving Chumbak, Alicia Souza had built her namesake creative business from scratch. It was small, cozy and just the right size—much like her favourite corner in the house where she sketched her whimsical drawings. Every morning, she'd sip her coffee, surrounded by her loving family (especially her dog Charlie!), and think about how lucky she was to do what she loved.

But as the orders grew and clients multiplied, so did the pressure. People constantly told her, 'This is your chance to expand! Grow bigger, hire more people!' Yet Alicia didn't want that. She loved the intimate feel of her business, knowing her customers personally, outsourcing parts of the work she knew others could do better and having time for herself while doing a variety of projects. She didn't want endless meetings or to become the kind of boss who was constantly chasing delivery deadlines as she liked to draw—and that is exactly what she wanted to focus on.

'I'm happy where we are,' she'd say to herself. 'More isn't always better.'

But then came the guilt. Should she be pushing harder? Everyone around her seemed to hustle, glorifying fourteen-hour workdays and late-night emails. Alicia, on the other hand, wanted evenings to herself. She wanted to play with her dog, chat with her partner, spend time with her toddler or just binge-watch a series without worrying about the next deadline!

For a while, she felt torn. Was she failing because she didn't want to scale her business into a mega-brand?

One evening, after an exhausting day of trying to keep up with everyone's expectations, she sat down with her sketchbook. The simple joy of drawing reminded her of why she started this in the first place. If she had continued with her last startup, the brand would have been bigger but maybe she wouldn't be having the balance she did now. Alicia realized that success doesn't look the same for everyone. Some thrive in chaos and ambition; others, like her, found fulfillment in balance.

She decided that it was okay to let go of the guilt. Her business didn't have to grow into something massive.

What mattered was that it brought her joy and gave her the freedom to live the life she wanted.

And maybe, just maybe, more people needed to hear this: it's perfectly fine not to work around the clock. It's okay if you don't want to grow endlessly. You're allowed to pause, breathe and choose balance over burnout. Life isn't a race and success isn't measured in exhaustion.

Sometimes, the bravest thing you can do is to say, 'This is enough.' And for Alicia, it truly was.

Looking back, Alicia reminisces how she was always the quiet one. In art school, while others were boisterous and eager to show off their work, Alicia preferred the background. Her sketchbook was her world, filled with quirky doodles and playful characters that reflected her inner thoughts—a language she could never quite speak out loud. She'd often sit in the corner, headphones on, drawing for hours, while the idea of presenting her work or talking about it made her stomach churn.

Cut to now when she is speaking at conferences and people relate to her quirky take on life—the everyday awkwardness, the little joys, the way she sees the world with humour and warmth. But success didn't change her overnight. Alicia is still introverted, still shy, but now there is a spark of confidence in her.

Alicia, once a wallflower in the art world, has become a well-known name. And as she has flourished, something amazing has happened—her introversion doesn't hold her back anymore. Instead, it has become her strength. She has learned that her thoughtful, introspective nature has allowed her to observe life in a way others miss. Her illustrations capture the humour and beauty in small, often overlooked moments.

As she spoke to us, Alicia felt a wave of pride, not just for her work, but for the journey she had taken. From the shy girl in the corner to a confident, opinionated artist who uses her voice—both through her work and her words—to connect with the world.

She didn't need to change who she was to find success. She had simply found a way to embrace it. And in doing so, she has inspired thousands of other quiet dreamers to realize that confidence doesn't always come from being the loudest in the room. Sometimes, it grows from being true to yourself.

From Being Lost to Being Limitless

Fifteen years ago, Nihal was a lost soul while he was sitting alone near his college's basketball court. He did not know what he wanted, and how to even begin. Uncertain about his future, he felt a deep sense of purposelessness. Today, he has been running Limitless Institute for over a decade. He is absolutely clear on his path. He mentions that even if the current version of Limitless goes bankrupt, he will start it again. Maybe he will do it in a different way, but he is clear there is nothing else he would rather be doing.

Nihal's transformation is a testament to the power of self-discovery and perseverance. Through introspection and exploration, he found his calling: to help others unlock their potential and live a purposeful life. Over the years, he has helped many become limitless, much like himself. Through its various programmes, the institute has directly reached over 20,000 individuals across every continent, empowering them to discover their passions, connect the dots and embark on fulfilling careers. There are many who were able to become entrepreneurs, change their career trajectory for the better, or start their dream projects, such as setting up a biogas plant in their village in South Africa.

The snowball effect of the work done by Limitless is far-reaching. Nihal has completed his journey from being a lost teenager to guiding others to newfound pursuits.

Exercise

Can you recall a time when your work led to a snowball effect? When did it happen? Where were you when it happened? How was the experience? Write a LinkedIn post about it.

Phani Finally Catches the Bus Home

Phani shares how, in the initial days as an entrepreneur, he used to micromanage his team for every small thing. Success meant so much that he thought with his energy and intelligence, he could pull everyone along and get them to do what was necessary.

As time passed, Phani went through myriad challenges along with his team. With scale, he realized that there is only so much you could do and the behaviour of a leader seeps down into the organization. The ego of a founder subsides with time, and one becomes reflective. Instead of pushing his ideas, he now wanted to put redBus and his team first. He started asking himself, 'Will this make redBus successful? What is the right thing to do for the long term? If not, whatever it takes for redBus to be successful, I will change.' The ego is replaced by the startup's goals and there is a sense of lightness in approaching one's work.

Phani shares how he started looking at the bigger picture, gradually letting his team take the lead.

Phani used to be, and possibly is even now, one of the smartest people in the room. But when it was the time to share ideas, he started listening more and guiding his team to shape them better. The desire to make redBus successful made him evolve into the wonderful human being he is today. He transformed into the humble, gentle person who went on to become Chief Innovation Officer of the Government of Telangana.

Phani shares how the journey of entrepreneurship has taught him that if an entrepreneur is selfish, he might not be able to scale. Running a startup is like playing an intense video game without ever so glancing up. If you keep playing it, you will lose sight of all that is happening around you. But if you keep your situational awareness intact, you will be able to achieve holistic growth, professionally and personally. With generosity, authenticity and openness, you will attract the right talent and collaborate to create value.

Good entrepreneurs live their values instead of wearing masks and piling on pressure on their teams. They show a vision and help the employees achieve that vision by helping them, gradually and with accountability. This takes a tremendous journey of self-understanding and evolution. While Phani knew his own ideas were great, he knew taking a step back would let redBus surge forward with a hundred steps.

What is interesting is that entrepreneurship puts you in those unique sets of circumstances where you have to make pertinent choices. For instance, Phani had to decide whether to take different commissions from different operators. This might sound like a business decision, but it actually is a decision for who you choose to be as a person. Entrepreneurship exposes you to a diverse range of people and perspectives. Developing empathy and emotional intelligence can improve your relationships, both personally and professionally—and it can set you on a journey of self-discovery.

Phanindra Sama, now an advisor to startups, philanthropist and content family man, looks back at his journey and shares how entrepreneurship is a way to seek answers and questions both, if you don't have them. Having put his skills to work on social innovation, he wants to contribute back to society. He is not in the race to be the biggest unicorn in the country but is happy to read stories of unicorns and mermaids to his children.

Phani smiles as he looks at the horizon. After having missed his bus for Diwali, he started redBus and exited, making it the biggest overseas strategic acquisition of an Indian Internet asset at that time. For Phani, the last twenty years have been a journey of growth and wisdom. And he is happy now he is spending his Diwali with his family, while creating magic in the startup ecosystem and giving back to society. He is happy that he does not have to miss a bus anymore.

* * *

'The journey of entrepreneurship is a process of self-purification,' Phanindra tells us, after having shared how he has lived the philosophy of his life by being a startup founder. The stories of all the entrepreneurs we spoke to merge at this focal point. While the entrepreneurial journey is an epic undertaking taken by anyone who chooses it, it's a profound journey of introspection that defines startup founders as individuals.

The hero's integration back into the ordinary world, with everything he or she has ever learned, is life coming full circle. It might seem that through the challenges, doubts, mysteries and victories, the startup comes to life, but it is actually the individual who gets polished into a better version of themselves. The startup is only a means to self-transformation and value creation.

And when they return to their origins with their hard-earned wisdom, the entrepreneurs are not the same anymore. Some become mentors, some start new journeys and some grow on to transform their environment for the better. It is often the starting of another journey, not just for themselves, but for many others—whether it is Frodo in *The Lord of the Rings*, Lord Rama returning to Ayodhya after vanquishing Ravana, Mother Teresa finding her calling to uplift the destitute of Kolkata or Mahatma Gandhi coming back to India to lead the fight for independence. And while it might seem like an end, another hero's journey begins.

Your Adventure Begins Now . . .

Acknowledgements

By Nitin

This book is not just a collection of words and stories—it's a tapestry woven from the love, resilience and encouragement of the people who have walked with me through life. I would like to acknowledge them here.

To Palak, my wife, my partner, my anchor—you've been the quiet force behind every word written and every moment of doubt conquered. When I was lost in a fog of uncertainty, you brought clarity, offering not just your encouragement but actionable solutions to pull me out of my writer's block. Who could have imagined that our two worlds—entrepreneurship and storytelling—would come together so beautifully in this journey? You are, and always will be, my greatest collaborator and the heart of this journey.

To my mother Bhagyawati, father Mahendra, and Neha and Khushal, your unwavering love and support have been the foundation upon which I have built everything in my life. The stability you have provided gave me the courage to take risks and fly without the fear of falling. Finishing this book by Mom's birthday was a little tribute to the quiet sacrifices and unspoken love you have given me every single day.

To my mentor Devashish, I still remember the day you sat across from me and asked, 'What if you pushed further?' That simple statement became the genesis of this book.

To my co-founders of Niki.ai—Keshav, Sachin and Shishir, you have been my heroes of a journey that we shared for seven years. Thank you for being there with me every step of the way.

To the entrepreneurs who generously shared their stories for this book and have inspired my life, thank you for your honesty and vulnerability. You've turned dreams into blueprints and struggles into lessons. This book is a testament to your courage and an ode to the relentless spirit of those who dare to follow their bliss.

To my second family in Surat, my friends Shivank and Bhanu, and every team member of Niki.ai, thank you all for being a part of this journey. This book is not just mine—it's ours.

To my co-author Prateek, right from our college days, I knew we would build a product together. But I never imagined that it would be in this form and shape. You were the first person I had in mind for the book, and I was over the moon when you came on board. Since then, over the last three years, our Wednesday and Saturday meetings have been a habit I have become fond of. I look forward to us having more adventures together!

Lastly, my sincere thanks to Radhika and Sakshi from Penguin Random House India. Your thoughtful feedback and guidance have been invaluable in refining and shaping this book.

By Prateek

I owe this playbook to all the heroes of my story who I am deeply grateful to.

To start with, every breath I take, I owe it to my parents. Baba for being my real-life hero. Wherever you are, I know you are Mawashi Geri, kicking demons like you always did for us. Thank you for getting me my *Amar Chitra Katha*s, even at the risk of missing trains. You will be my first and last hero always!

Maa, for making me believe that heroes are not always men and strength comes from persistence, resilience and fighting for family and not just having the die of destiny cast in your favour. You are the moon that brought out the tsunami of writing in me and you are the driving force that shaped who I am today. I can't ever thank you enough for what you have done for me and I place this book at your feet.

Appa, for being the Gandalf, Yoda and Chanakya of my life. My deepest gratitude for introducing me to Joseph Campbell's writings with a book gifted on my birthday. You were the guide that helped me enter the dark caves that held the treasure I sought and this book is a small step. Your light shines bright in dark places and I wouldn't be where I am today without you. Big hugs.

Shweta, my sister, for seeing me as a writer long ago, pushing me to do something out of the ordinary, jamming on ideas for the book and being the sibling to be published first. Thank you for always challenging me and being my lucky stone. Forever with you chasing butterflies in Mpen!

Bhumika, my love. For believing in me. Right after six months of getting married, I started this book. It wouldn't have been published today if not for your consistent encouragement, sacrifice and generosity of time over many weekends, which I spent writing it out. Thank you for the ginger tea, filter coffee, fresh ideas and for being my sunshine on rainy days. Look, we did it!

Babel, well, look where we are. But we wouldn't be here if you had not called me that fateful day with the idea of writing a book. It would always have been a romantic notion. Thank you for pushing me, challenging me and being the yin to the yang in this epic journey, old friend.

Radhika and Sakshi, the best publishers that could ever be, for believing in us—first-time authors—and proving to be allies in our heroic endeavour.

Scan QR code to access the
Penguin Random House India website